Barbed Wire and Bamboo

Barbed Wire and Bamboo

Australian POWs in Europe, North Africa, Singapore, Thailand and Japan

Hugh V. Clarke and Colin Burgess

Allen & Unwin

First published in 1992
First published in paperback 1993
Allen & Unwin Pty Ltd
9 Atchison Street, St Leonards, NSW 2065 Australia

National Library of Australia
Cataloguing-in-Publication entry:

Clarke, Hugh V. (Hugh Vincent), 1919– .
Barbed wire and bamboo: Australian POWs in Europe,
North Africa, Singapore, Thailand and Japan.

ISBN 1 86373 421 X

1. World War, 1939–1945—Europe—Prisoners and prisons.
2. World War, 1939–1945—East Asia—Prisoners and prisons.
3. Prisoners of war—Australia.   4. Prisoners of war—Europe.
5. Prisoners of war—East Asia.   I. Burgess, Colin, 1947– .
II. Title.

940.547

Cover photographs
left: German guards at Stalag VIII B,
Lamsdorf, searching a work party.
(British Red Cross Museum and Archives)
right: Japanese guards pose
at a work party site (Imperial
War Museum, London HU6352).

Maps on pages xx–xxiii by Valda Brook
Illustrations on pages xxiv and 106 by Verdon Morcom

Set in 11 on 14 pt Palatino
by Graphicraft Typesetters Ltd, Hong Kong
Printed by South Wind Production, Singapore

1 2 3 4 5 6 7 8 9 10

Contents

Contents

Authors' note

THE title of this book is derived from the name of the official publication of the Ex-Prisoners of War Association whose members have been a major source for many of the stories in this book.

It is intended as a tribute to the Association and its members, living and dead.

Colin Burgess is responsible for the European prisoners of war section of the book and Hugh Clarke for stories about prisoners of the Japanese.

Preface
by Colin Burgess

I N prefacing the many remarkable stories told in this book, it should be pointed out that readers may notice a difference in writing styles between the two authors. For just as surely as the stories are presented against a grim backdrop of widely varying geographical and cultural settings, so too the authors came to this project as willing and friendly collaborators from different generations of Australians, with different backgrounds and perspectives and experiences—not the least being that Hugh was an actual participant in some of the events described in this book, while I am a postwar chronicler, who has never been to war.

Hugh Clarke was born in a country town near Brisbane in 1919, the son of a prosperous publican who like many others in Australia in the late 1920s fell victim to the heartless wrath of the Depression. The Clarke family knew the hard times of those terrible years but in spite of the hardships this national calamity somehow exerted a unifying influence that was to remain within the men and women of Australia during the Second World War. Hugh left a cadetship in surveying with the Queensland Main Roads Commission to enlist in the 2/10th Field Regiment, 8th Division, in July 1940. He served as a bombardier in Malaya and Singapore, and as a prisoner of the Japanese survived such inhumanities and terrors as those of Changi and Hell Fire Pass on the Burma–Thailand railway—the railway of death which over the worst sections claimed a life for every sleeper. Liberation came to Hugh as he worked in a timber yard in Fukuoka, having been sent to Japan to work with other prisoners of war. The atom bombs unleashed on Hiroshima and Nagasaki put an end to the war with Japan and he returned home—only to learn that his younger brother Danny had been killed two years before while serving in the RAF.

Hugh has written six books about his prisoner of war experiences and those of his mates, and is a well-known author on the subject. Long before I had the great pleasure of meeting Hugh I knew of him through his books, and the friendship I share with Hugh and his family these days is a privilege I treasure. My own credentials are far less tumultuous; I was born in Sydney in 1947 and was raised in that postwar period characterised by an intense spirit of growth and optimism.

My father never went to war; his enthusiasm was dashed by a hearing ailment, and I cannot lay claim to any close relative having been a prisoner of war. The question invariably rises: why such an interest in prisoners of war? The answer, to me, is quite simple, and harks back to my childhood. That first decade after the war saw a profusion of POW and escape literature which found a permanent place on many library shelves; at school, my peers and I found nail-biting excitement and high drama in such classics as *The Wooden Horse, The Great Escape* and *The Colditz Story*. I began to haunt secondhand book shops, buying up escape literature in those delightful paperback editions with the evocative illustrations on their covers. I even dared to write to some of the authors, care of their publishers, and received some much-prized replies from men I regarded (and still do) as great heroes.

That, in a nutshell, is how I came to be interested in POW literature. Then, in England in 1981, I finally met a man I'd admired for years, and who was to give me a whole new direction in life. His name was Patrick Robert Reid, the distinguished author of *The Colditz Story*, and it was he who urged me to research and write a book about the Australians who'd wound up in the infamous castle prison. The result, four years later, was *The Diggers of Colditz*, which I proudly co-authored with ex-Colditz veteran Jack Champ from Geelong in Victoria.

These days I am in contact with former POWs from all over Australia and the world, and I am finding myself increasingly entrusted with their war stories from the European theatre— some written painstakingly in longhand, others carefully compiled on word processors, but each imbued with something very special. They are the stories of men suddenly wrenched away from their homes and loved ones, facing uncertain futures in a world dominated by stony-faced guards and barbed wire; sharing with other hungry men the sparse and unnourishing rations which had to be measured and treasured by the milligram. They are stories of small personal triumphs and horrifying tragedies which were part and parcel of everyday life for the prisoner of war in Europe. These young men had to learn to be tolerant of their fellow human beings in an alien world of filth, hunger, disease, death and uncertainty. That so many of them returned home in many ways better for their experience is a great and lasting tribute to the temerity and defiance of the Australian serviceman and his Allied counterparts.

A former prisoner of war and long-time friend Mike Moran once expressed to me how he felt in looking back at those endless years of captivity in Germany:

The French have a phrase, '*la nostalgie d'hier*', and as one grows older one's understanding of that sentiment becomes more and more clear. The memories and experiences of our yesterdays are the basis on which many of us live our todays. The companionship, the shared loyalties, the standards we held so dear, the men who were our particular chums—these are all part of the nostalgia as, indeed, is the awareness that as young men we were privileged. Life did not pass us by as it might have done had we belonged to another generation. The nettle was there to grasp; it had been placed within our reach. But its stings, for most of us, had no lasting ability to hurt. Rather, with the passing of the years they became an enrichment to our lives.

Some years back I wrote to the editor of the ex-POW Association magazine *Barbed Wire and Bamboo*, asking for any of its readers who had been held prisoner in Europe to send me their stories; I was quite overwhelmed by the volume and standard of the response. Many of those stories are told within this book.

The inherent sadness is that for every one of these remarkable stories I am privileged to record, hundreds of others go untold. Families of former prisoners who have passed away show me shoeboxes of dog-eared black and white photos which had been the property of their loved one. There are generally few notations on the back of these photographs; the stories they tell will be lost forever within a generation or two, and many will end up unwanted and ultimately discarded. Those photographs and lovingly compiled war diaries and letters home are ineluctably yellowing with age; so too are there fewer and fewer ex-POWs gathering at the various reunions. I trust we will never know a war such as the two World Wars again, and it is my belief that we should all make an endeavour to listen to, and learn from, a generation of men and women who experienced it in so many different ways. If we are to know something of the future we must look to the past.

Hugh Clarke writes with the compassion, conviction and insight of a person who was there; one who cried tears of frustration working on the hell that was the Burma–Thailand railway as his mates fell or were hammered unmercifully to the ground and died around him—and who has survived to tell the story. His empathetic and well-chosen stories, some written directly about his own experiences and others incorporating the recollections of fellow POWs, are therefore told in a style befitting that of eyewitnesses to one of life's most reviled and horrific episodes.

I write as someone who has never known the vicissitudes and horrors of war, but as a member of that postwar 'baby boom' generation who fully realises and appreciates the incredible debt we owe such men and women, and who has nothing but the highest respect and admiration for these fine people of my parents' generation. My style therefore is that of the chronicler eager to preserve the stories of our servicemen and women, and therefore they are recounted in the third person. Several of the more outstanding or poignant incidents fully deserve to be told in the words of the subjects themselves, and these personal vignettes are peppered throughout the accounts.

The difference in the manner in which Hugh and I have tackled the stories in this book may indeed create a somewhat ragged amalgam of writing styles, and for this we beg the readers' indulgence. Perhaps we could have found a middle road and adapted to each other's way of writing, but ultimately we decided to scribe from the heart, in the way we each know best.

Judge this book then not by its stylistic diversity. Judge it by the sheer, compelling nature of the stories within—some short, some quite lengthy, but each infused with the souls of some quite ordinary men who lived, and oft-times died, enmeshed in barbed wire and bamboo.

> The years we thought would never end,
> When hopes were food and dreams were wine,
> When dismal dreary fate would lend
> Despair to every essayed line.
>
> Those days are gone—with youth they've fled
> Across some distant far-flung sky,
> A sky uncharted, dim, unknown,
> Where years once lived steal off to die.
>
> Mike Moran, 1945

Introduction
by Hugh Clarke

A T the outbreak of World War II on 3 September 1939 Australians in their thousands flocked to join the AIF, the RAAF and the RAN. The dismal years of the Great Depression had almost faded and the prospect of sailing to distant lands to fight for king and country was a beckoning adventure not to be missed.

Soon the troopships began sailing to Palestine and in June 1940 the entry of Italy into the war transformed the Middle East from a training ground into a theatre of active operations. By the end of the year the 6th and 7th Divisions were in the Middle East and a third division—the 8th—was formed in early 1941 to go to Malaya. The 9th Division was formed in the Middle East around a nucleus of 6th Division troops who had been diverted to England during the previous June. Meanwhile airmen and sailors were already serving in the various far-flung battle arenas.

New placenames began taking over Australian headlines— Bardia, Derna, Tobruk, Benghazi, Alamein, Greece, Crete and Syria. Australian troops in Malaya fumed impotently as they read about battles in the desert and elsewhere and had no doubt that they would never see action in the jungles of Malaya.

But fighting or waiting, into every man's mind at some time or other came a thought of the possibilities. One might be killed or wounded and possibly maimed for life. Usually though that sort of disaster happened to the other bloke. The one possibility almost nobody considered, except perhaps airmen who were accustomed to flying over enemy territory, was captivity. In time the grim facts were to become the source of innumerable books including this one.

Australian prisoners of war in Germany and Italy numbered 7116 of whom 582 were successful in escaping and 242 died in captivity. Of Australians taken prisoner by the Japanese more than one-third died in captivity—in all 7777. Of these 27 were executed for attempted escape and 193 for other reasons. Only 25 men succeeded in escaping from the Japanese—from Ambon and Borneo.

By comparison, of 18 432 Italian prisoners of war held in Australia, 101 died and of 1658 Germans, eight died. Of 5637 Japanese prisoners of war held in Australia a total of 314 died including 231 deaths as a result of the outbreak at Cowra and 43 suicides.

These statistics reflect the attitudes of the respective captors to their captives. The Germans and Italians accepted the fact that it was a prisoner's duty to try to escape and, generally, observed the rules of civilised warfare towards their captives. The average Allied airman, soldier or sailor, on his part, looked upon his presence in an enemy prisoner of war camp as a piece of the blackest bad luck. To him it was not so much a cause of personal shame as a spur to cast off a temporary irksome restraint as the opportunity occurred. He devoted an incredible degree of organisation, cunning and patience to the creation of such opportunities.

The Germans and Italians, generally, ran their prisoner of war camps as close as possible to the provisions of the Geneva Convention. This agreement had been made in 1929 and ratified by Hitler in 1934 and it stipulated that prisoners of war should be placed under the control of the corresponding arm of the enemy's service as the one to which they belonged.

It also provided for the inspection of camps by so-called

Protecting Powers whose duty it was to ensure that the humanities were observed. In Germany the Swiss looked after the British, American and De-Gaullist French prisoners; the Petain Government looked after the French; the Swedish Government looked after the Dutch; and the International Red Cross the Poles.

The attitude of the Japanese authorities in charge of prisoner of war camps extending from Changi to Rangoon was quite different from that of the Allied powers or the Germans. As Japan had not been a signatory to the Geneva Convention, the rules in Japanese prisoner of war camps varied from place to place and in most instances depended on the individual officer in charge. Thus the treatment meted out to prisoners varied greatly. In addition, the average Japanese soldier's belief in the shame and hopelessness of captivity had been so inculcated in him that his attitude to prisoners was basically one of contempt, disregard or outright hostility.

On one point however there was consistency and that was the official Japanese attitude to prisoners attempting escape. On 23 August 1942 Major General Fukuye, Commander of Changi prisoner of war camp issued an order that all prisoners were to sign the following statement: 'I, the undersigned, hereby solemnly swear that I will not, under any circumstances, attempt escape'.

All Australian and British prisoners in the camp refused to sign and three days later the Japanese executed four men who had previously tried to escape and insisted on the senior Allied commanders witnessing the executions. In a volume of the Australian official war history, *The Japanese Thrust*, the incident is described:

The four men executed included two Australians, Corporal B.E. Breavington and Private V.L. Gale who had escaped from a camp at Bukit Timah (Singapore) on 12 May 1942, obtained a small boat and rowed it about 200 miles to the island of Colombo. There in semi-starved condition they had been re-arrested and at length returned to Singapore where Breavington was admitted to hospital suffering from malaria.

At the execution ground Breavington, the older man, made an appeal to the Japanese to spare Gale. He said he had ordered Gale to escape and that Gale had merely obeyed orders; this appeal was refused. As the Sikh firing party knelt before the doomed men, the British officers present saluted and the men returned the salute. Breavington walked to the others and shook hands with them. A Japanese Lieutenant then came forward with a handkerchief and offered it to Breavington who waved it aside with a smile and the offer was refused by all men. Breavington then called to one of the padres present and asked for a new testament whence he read a short passage. Thereupon the order was given by the Japanese to fire.

Thus was established the inflexible Japanese attitude to attempted escapes. The Germans on the other hand extended at least a sporting chance to enterprising prisoners of war.

During World War I in which some 4000 Australians were taken prisoner by the Germans the impact of their captivity on the Australian public was overshadowed and dimmed by the enormity of the 60 000 dead. Nevertheless the experiences of the prisoners taken were not so dissimilar to those of World War II prisoners.

In the early years of World War II the remoteness of the fields of battle softened the impact of prisoner of war reports on the Australian public until the Japanese, like a whirlwind, brought the war to our doorstep.

The news of the fall of the 'impregnable' fortress of Singapore on 15 February 1942 reverberated around the world and the capture of 15 384 Australians brought a sudden and new meaning of the term 'prisoner of war' to the stunned Australian public.

The shock did not end with Singapore as more and more Australians were captured during the early months of 1942— 2736 in Java, 1137 in Timor, 1075 in Ambon and 1049 in New Britain.

In addition, for the first time in our history the shadow of enemy invasion hung over our northern shores. Darwin and Broome were bombed and enemy submarines penetrated Sydney Harbour.

It is therefore not surprising that most of the postwar writing on recent military history became bound up with the Japanese and the experiences of their prisoners of war.

This book seeks to redress this imbalance somewhat by devoting the greater part to stories of Australians who fell into German and Italian hands. These stories are told partly in the former prisoners' own words and reveal an incredible record of courage, endurance, enterprise and stoicism. The outstanding feature of captivity in German and Italian hands was the dedication of so many prisoners of war to the aim of escaping.

For prisoners of the Japanese escape was a far less achievable ambition so that the theme of most of their stories are mateship, endurance and survival as exemplified in Gunner Kitch Loughnan's account of the sinking of the prison ship *Rokyu Maru* on its voyage to Japan in 1944.

Each story has its own particular theme such as the chapter on the Fall of Singapore which could easily have served as a case history in Norman F. Dixson's memorable book *On the Psychology of Military Incompetence*.

Maps

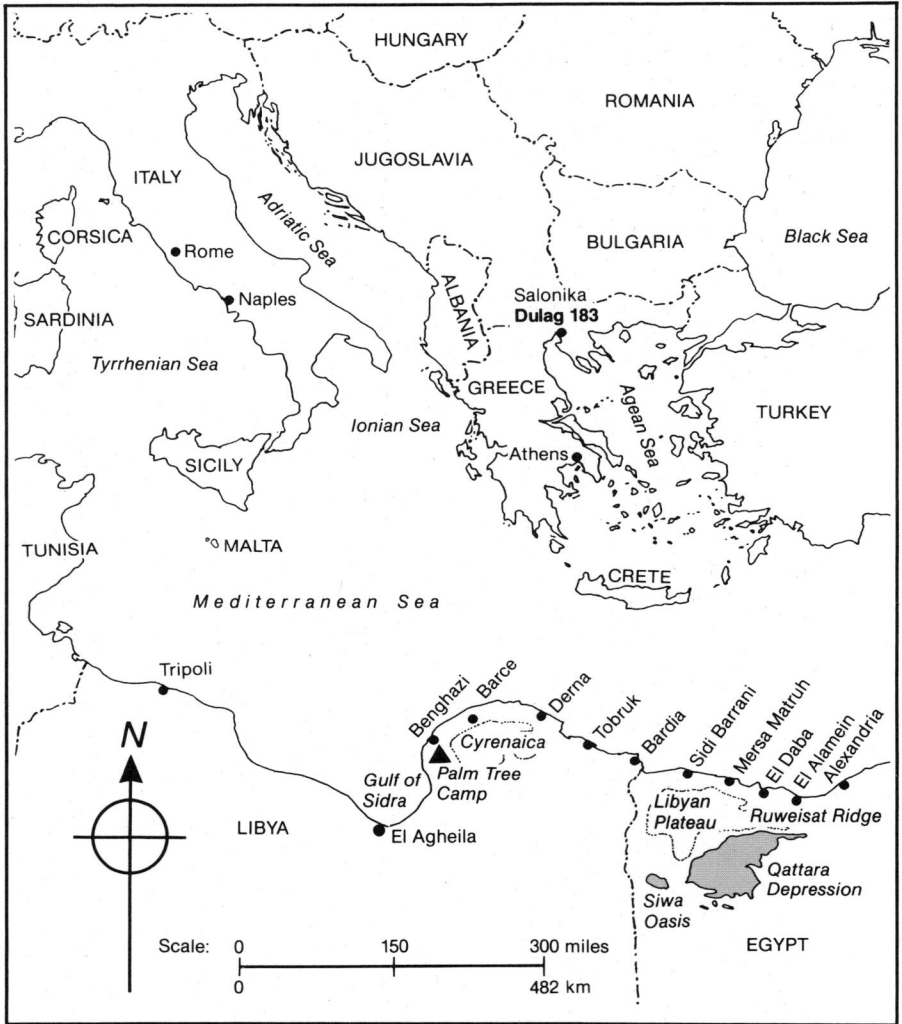

German boundary, 1937
German boundary, 1942
Concentration camps
POW camps
Cities, towns in text

SWEDEN

DENMARK

Baltic Sea

North Sea

Barth (Luft I)

Gross Tychow
(Luft IV)

Hamburg

Bremen

Melbeck
Soltau

BERLIN

POLAND

Hanover

GERMANY

Dobrilugk-
Kirchain
Sagan (Luft III)

Dusseldorf

Leipzig

Bad Sulza (IXC)
Buchenwald
Weimar   Molsdorf

Dresden

Breslau

Colditz
(Oflag IVC)

Lamsdorf
(VIIIB)

NETHERLANDS

BELGIUM

Oberursel
(Dulag Luft)
Frankfurt

Theresienstadt

BOHEMIA   Prague

CZECHOSLOVAKIA

Luxembourg

Nuremberg

Brno

Eichstatt (VIIB)
Moosburg (VIIA)
Munich

Vienna

FRANCE

AUSTRIA

LEICHTENSTEIN
Berne
SWITZERLAND

Wolfsberg (XVIIIA)
Klagenfurt

Gruppignano
(PG57)

ITALY

Scale: 0   100 miles

0   161 km

Bologna
(PG19)

*Adriatic
Sea*

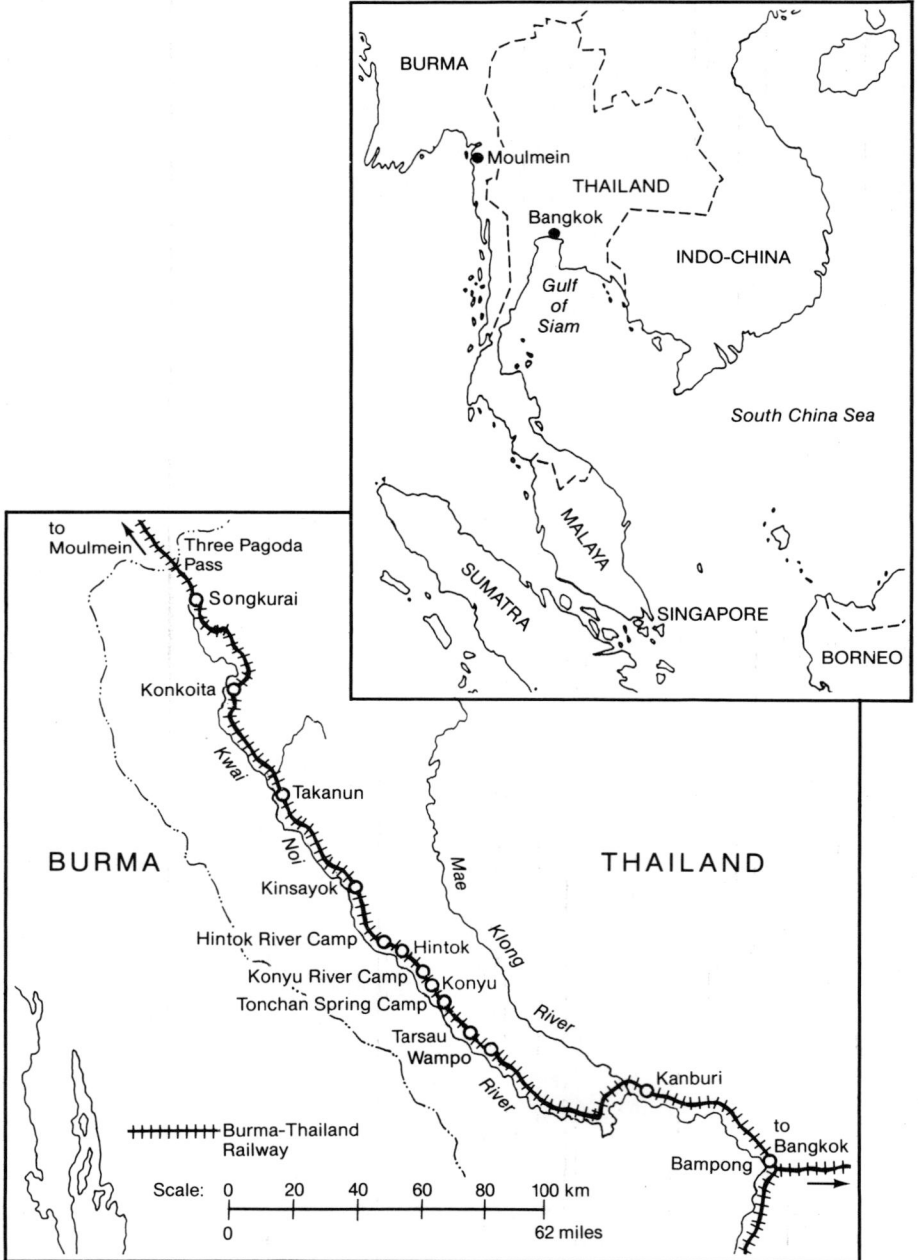

BURMA

Moulmein

THAILAND

Bangkok

INDO-CHINA

*Gulf
of
Siam*

South China Sea

SUMATRA

MALAYA

SINGAPORE

BORNEO

to
Moulmein

Three Pagoda
Pass

Songkurai

Konkoita

Kwai

Takanun

Noi

Kinsayok

BURMA

Hintok River Camp

Hintok

Konyu River Camp

Konyu

Tonchan Spring Camp

Tarsau

Wampo

Mae

Klong

River

THAILAND

Kanburi

River

to
Bangkok

Bampong

++++++++ Burma-Thailand
Railway

Scale: 0   20   40   60   80   100 km

0   62 miles

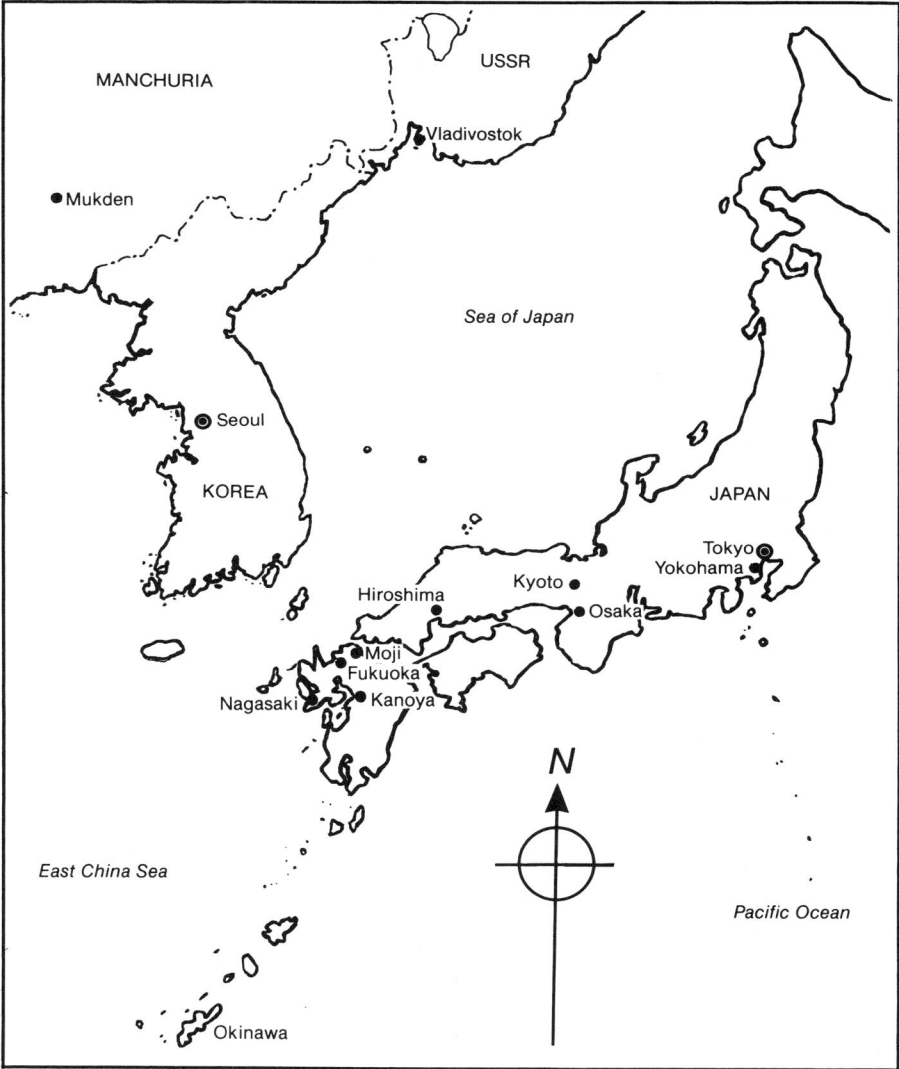

MANCHURIA

USSR

● Vladivostok

● Mukden

Sea of Japan

◎ Seoul

KOREA

JAPAN

Tokyo ◎
Yokohama ●

Kyoto ●

Hiroshima ●

Osaka ●

● Moji
Fukuoka

Nagasaki ● Kanoya

East China Sea

N

Pacific Ocean

Okinawa

Part I
Australian POWs in Europe and North Africa

1

The Great War

O N 4 August 1914, Great Britain declared war on Germany and the Austrian Empire following their deliberate violation of Belgian neutrality. Russia and France had already declared themselves at war with the Central Powers—Germany, Austria–Hungary, Turkey and Bulgaria.

Almost immediately the entire British Empire was mobilised. Australia's and New Zealand's 1st Divisions, plus the Australian 4th Brigade, were dispatched to Egypt where they completed their training. Recruiting began in earnest when the Prime Minister, Mr Fisher, declared that Australia 'would send the last man and spend the last shilling if need be'. By Armistice Day in November 1918, the Australian forces had suffered 211 513 casualties from a total enlistment of 331 781. Of these 61 862 had paid the supreme sacrifice. As well, 4084 soldiers of the Australian Imperial Forces were taken prisoner.

Don Fraser was oyster farming on the reaches of the lower Macleay River in New South Wales when he decided to join up. He filled in the necessary papers at Kempsey on 1 June 1915, and after passing his medical the twenty-year-old was accepted into his country's armed forces. Training done, he joined the 7th Reinforcements of the 13th Infantry Battalion.

He saw service in Gallipoli, was evacuated in the clandestine withdrawal on 20 December 1915, and after a short spell in

England was sent to France. Don Fraser was captured in a combined assault on the Hindenburg Line by the 16th and 13th Battalions on 11 April 1917. Wounded in both arms, he was sent by train to a German hospital in Munster, where he was pleased to meet several of his friends. From there, the men were eventually dispatched to Soltau, the main internment camp.

On arrival at Soltau the prisoners were placed in long army huts, and given two very thin single blankets and a sack of straw to lay on during the night. One of their own sergeants was placed in each hut. Much to everyone's relief, the men were issued with Red Cross food, which Fraser says saved them from the expected fate of death due to starvation. He recalled:

> Soltau was a real league of nations. I think every nation which was at war with Germany was represented there—Russians, French, Belgian, Italian, Serbians, Rumanians, and just about every regiment in the British Army. There were thousands of Russians. The Germans treated them frightfully badly. They were dying at the rate of five or six a day. During my stay there, they used to carry the bodies out in a box, tip it into a hole, and then go back for the next one.

After several weeks at Soltau, Fraser, together with ten other Australians and an Englishman, were sent on a work detail to the Kieselgour Works, near Melbeck. Here they were employed in mining and drying a light clay substance which they subsequently learnt was used as a binding element for nitroglycerine. Fraser made one escape from the works in the company of three Australians, but they were recaptured while attempting to communicate with some British prisoners on a hay-gathering detail. They were escorted back to their camp and thrown into solitary confinement cells for fourteen days. The floors of the small cells were to be their beds, with blocks of wood provided as pillows. Every fourth day the guards opened the cells' steel shutters, allowing the sun to stream in, which was some small comfort after the darkness which had prevailed. On this day the prisoners would also be given a bowl of sauerkraut. The sole meal on other days comprised two thin slices of sour black bread and water. 'It was the longest fourteen days I have ever spent in my life', Fraser recalled.

When their period of solitary confinement was over, Fraser and the other three escapers, 'Yank' Buchanan, Arthur Greasley and 'Scottie' Young, were assembled in a hall and given a lecture on the folly of escape by the prison's *Hauptman* (captain). Following this the men were told that they were being returned to the Kieselgour Works, and warned not to attempt another escape.

On arrival back at Melbeck the four men were extremely weak after their ordeal in the cells, but their mates had some tinned meat, biscuits and tea which they shared with them. After their recent starvation diet the rich food was marvellous, and tasted wonderful going down. Unfortunately their stomachs were so weak that in very short order they were bringing it all back up again. The four men gradually recovered, and slowly returned to the delights of their Australian Red Cross parcels.

The manager of the works and his engineer lived in a large house 50 metres from the prisoners' quarters, and the engineer had a young teenage son who used to hang around the Australians. After a little prompting he shyly explained that he wanted to learn to speak English. Arthur Greasly had spent some time going to school with a German family back in prewar Queensland, and had picked up a useful amount of the language, so he and Don Fraser volunteered to teach the lad a few English phrases. Fraser confided:

> All we actually taught the boy was a very descriptive vocabulary of swear words, and he would walk around all day repeating them, much to the delight of the men. I recall one day he poked his head around the corner of our hut and yelled at the top of his voice 'Get out you square-headed bastards!' He then looked at Arthur and me and said '*Ich good Englisch sprechen?*' [sic] To which we looked all suitably serious and replied '*Yah, yah, sehr gut!*' [sic]

Winter set in, and without the aid of the sun to dry the glutinous clay, several of the prisoners were dispatched to other working parties. Six, including Don Fraser, were escorted to a train—destination unknown. After a lengthy journey Fraser and the others could see chimney stacks. Jack Faull, a miner from Western Australia, informed his companions that it looked very much to him that they would all soon be working in a mine. None of the men fancied working underground, and they quickly discussed a plan to overpower the sentry on the train and escape. Jack Faull, who at 35 was considerably older than his companions, talked them out of their 'do or die' plan. He told the men that he'd worked in mines for most of his life, and that it might not be as bad as they imagined.

The train pulled into a rail siding at Kleine Hostlingen and the contingent of prisoners was hustled out of the trucks and marched into the compound of what proved to be a salt mine. There were many prisoners in the compound already, mainly Russians, but with a scattering of French and Belgians as well. Fraser's group were the first British or Australian prisoners to arrive at the working camp, and they became the object of curiosity for some time. The prisoners were quartered in some old stables—long buildings, once used to house the ponies which had pulled the trucks underground prior to the war. Now, electric motors or POWs were used instead. The new arrivals were given the usual bag of straw and double-decker bunks. Nearly 50 prisoners were housed in their particular stable, as Fraser recalls. He described a typical day's work in the mines:

On arriving at the top of the shaft we were hustled into a lift cage, a dozen at a time. We were then lowered 450 metres. The air was stifling hot on the bottom. We were then sent into different tunnels. My group were escorted along a drive for about half a mile. This was the most unbearable and hottest place in the mines, which was known as Ammonia Drive. Air had to be pumped down from the top. Without it we never would have survived. Two German miners worked at the face, boring holes so that they could dynamite the salt, which we then had to load into trucks, which ran on a light railway out to the bottom of the shaft, where they were pushed into the cage and sent to the surface.

A typical work day for the prisoners started at 6.00 a.m. and continued until 10.00 a.m. when they were given half-an-hour's rest. The miners used this half-hour to dynamite the face of the mine. Working conditions were much tougher after the series of blasts, as a choking mist of fine salt lingered in the air, and the heat was awful, while the pervasive smell of the explosives added to the general discomfort. The men worked on, wearing just trousers and boots, until 2.30 p.m. when they were finished for the day. At this time they made their way to the surface and headed straight for the shower room. 'This was the only pleasant part of the whole business—beautiful warm showers and clean clothes', said Fraser.

During Don Fraser's third week in the Ammonia Drive a bad accident occurred during their half-hour 'smoko' break. The German miners had laid several charges of dynamite, which they counted off as they exploded. When the noise from the final explosion had died down they shook their heads; one charge had failed to explode. The German who had laid the dynamite allowed a little time, then with his colleague in tow went down to where the charges had been placed into the walls, carefully checking the mine face with his miner's lamp. Suddenly the charge exploded, and the miner was instantly buried amid a shower of rock salt and thick, impenetrable dust. His companion, dazed and bleeding, rushed back to the safety zone crying *'Mein Kamerad, mein Kamerad!'* Fraser and the other prisoners rushed into the shaft and made their way to where the explosion had occurred. They soon located the miner, trapped beneath huge lumps of rock salt, with one large boulder resting on his head. Fortunately this rock had come to rest on top of another, otherwise it would have crushed his skull as easily as it would an egg shell. One leg was sticking out through the dust and rubble, and Fraser quickly saw that it had sustained a bad compound fracture, the bone easily visible as it protruded through the torn flesh and muscle above the knee. The man was in a bad way, and had slipped into shock.

Don Fraser and Arthur Greasly stood on either side of the huge rock and managed to lift it with considerable difficulty, but once it was free they were able to move the unconscious German. They loaded him onto a trolley which they hurriedly pushed along to the shaft, and from there he was taken up to the surface in the lift cage, accompanied by his companion. As they sat recovering from the ordeal, Fraser and Greasly discussed the man's injuries. They decided he didn't stand much of a chance of survival. Fraser recalled:

> However, one Sunday afternoon about three months later, the guard said we had a visitor who wished to see us. Sure enough, it was him with an iron on his leg and a walking stick. He came to thank us for getting him out. Evidently the doctor had told him that our quick action had saved his life.

The following day, after nearly a year in the salt mine, Fraser and the others in his group were moved out of the Ammonia Drive and onto less demanding salt-loading duties on the surface. They still worked hard, but at least they did not have to venture below ground again.

Freedom only came for Don Fraser and the others with the signing of the Armistice on 11 November 1918.

Opportunities to escape from the enemy occurred unexpectedly, and a plucky lance corporal from Queensland's Logan District was quick to seize his chance. He was, after all, 'just doing my duty' in his bold bid for freedom.

Born at Yatala in October 1895, Frederick Isaac Peachey enlisted in January 1916 and left Queensland for the battlefields of France on 16 May. He served with the 47th Battalion, 4th Division of the 1st AIF, until his capture at Dernacourt two years later on 5 April 1918. Strong German forces had breached the Allied lines near Amiens, and Fred Peachey was one of the reinforcement task group sent to hold the line until the Allied forces could be reorganised. A group of them were surrounded by the Germans and taken prisoner.

The first prison camp he and his mates were held in was located near the French village of Etricourt, positioned about 60 kilometres on the German side of the front line. It was from there that Peachey made his desperate bid to return to the Allied lines.

With the help of a fellow prisoner he slipped away from a water detail one evening, taking cover in a nearby wood until it was dark enough to move out. For the next three days he headed for the front line, travelling cautiously by night, dodging enemy patrols and zigzagging to avoid gun emplacements, hiding up by day. On the morning of the third day he passed through the German support line and came perilously close to being discovered by some fatigued enemy soldiers returning from the front-line trenches. He quickly scampered to the back of a nearby hill and found a large shell hole at the top in which to hide until darkness prevailed again. After planning the best place to cross the trench, he fell asleep for about an hour.

As Peachey slept a dense fog descended upon the area, and when he woke he was trembling from the cold and was mentally exhausted. Just as he was considering making a bolt across the German front-line trenches a one-man patrol appeared out of the fog and spotted the Allied uniform. Fred Peachey was taken at gun point, and found himself being marched through the enemy trenches, into the hessian-covered German headquarters. There an officer, who spoke good English, questioned the hapless Australian and then informed him he would be shot. Peachey argued that it was his duty to try to make it to his lines, that he was hungry, and that German prisoners in England were not only well looked after, but enjoyed good conditions and meals.

'You have seen this?' queried the officer. He listened with increasing interest as the Queenslander described a visit to a cousin's farm in England while on leave, where he had seen unguarded German prisoners assisting with the farm work. The two men talked about prisoners and food for some time. At one stage Peachey mentioned one of his reasons for escaping was that he was hungry, and even craved some of the ubiquitous British Bully Beef. The German did not understand the term 'Bully Beef' and repeated it several times. Peachey described the beef product so well known to Allied soldiers, and explained that it came in small tins with a picture of a bull's head on the can—hence the name 'Bully Beef'. The officer regretted he had none of the mysterious tinned beef to give Peachey, and blamed the *'verdammt'* British blockade for the overall lack of food supplies at the front. 'We cannot give you what we do not have', he stated firmly but sympathetically. Their conversation finally at an end, the officer had a guard take Peachey to a nearby prison camp, where he was blithely informed by an indifferent corporal that he was to be shot by a squad of British soldiers!

Peachey was held in an isolation cell under strict supervision for the remainder of that day and night. Towards morning he heard a nearby bombardment, but fell asleep once again until woken by the sentry just before daylight. The German explained that it had been a British bombardment, and that the prisoners were to be moved out. The threat of shooting had therefore proved to be an empty intimidation, for which Peachey was thankful, but he was doubly relieved to see that the guard had brought him some food—the first he had received since being recaptured. It was a simple piece of rye bread and a cup of lukewarm artificial coffee from the guard's own dixie, but food had never tasted better.

Soon after the camp was on the march, and later that day they reached the bomb-devastated town of Peronne, where the main column of prisoners were permitted to rest on a small grassed area in the town square. Peachey, with his personal escort of two sentries and a sergeant major, was ordered to remain standing. Two high-ranking officers, including a Prussian, who had been in charge of the column came forward and handed the prisoners over to another officer wearing Saxon colours on his tunic. After a while it became evident they were discussing procedures in regard to the recaptured Australian prisoner, as they kept pointing to Peachey. He remembered:

> Suddenly the Saxon officer spoke in harsh tones to the Prussian who saluted, clicked his heels, and said *'Jawohl!'*, before marching away. The Saxon beckoned that my escort and I come towards him. When we had reached a point about three paces from him he cried *'Halt!'* and put up one hand. Then he just looked straight at my face, and I looked steadily into his eyes for about a minute. Neither of us was going to be the first to look away, but eventually he pointed to where the other prisoners were sitting and ordered me to join them. From then on the sentries seemed to be keeping a special watch on me.

Eventually the prisoners reached their camp, situated well back from the war zone, in Alsace–Lorraine. This prison was quite crowded, and the sleeping quarters were located in a long, roomless building which had previously been used as a prison factory. Small barred windows high in the walls gave very little ventilation, and to exacerbate the general discomfort the toilets were located at either end of the building. These open toilet cubicles were in constant use day and night, and the fetid smell within the locked building was revolting. Many of the prisoners were ill, and the putrid, stuffy conditions assisted in quickly spreading a variety of serious diseases throughout the crowded building. It wasn't too long before Fred Peachey fell ill with double pneumonia, and became so weak that he was taken to the prison hospital, where he lay unconscious for three days.

The medical staff tended his illness with compassion, and it was with some reluctance they declared him fit once again a few weeks later. On his return to the prison Peachey found that the Germans were moving most of the four or five hundred prisoners to Russia, but sent Peachey and about 30 others to a smaller prison camp where there was a hospital for horses! The duties there were mostly to help the German staff care for the wounded or ill horses, while Fred Peachey found himself as an assistant to a carpenter doing rough building work and odd jobs.

The conditions at this camp were far better that those at the crowded prison, and the handful of prisoners lived in small huts similar to those of their guards, albeit surrounded by barbed-wire barricades. Peachey remained there until the signing of the Armistice. 'I took it hard being a prisoner', Fred Peachey stated, recalling some of the great privations he had suffered at the hands of the Kaiser's men. 'I chaffed the whole time until we were liberated, and abhorred being a prisoner of the German army.'

2

Terror in the mines

A S in the Great War, non-commissioned officers in the Second World War were required to do manual labour for their captors, under agreements reached as part of the Geneva Convention. This work was not supposed to be any kind which aided the enemy's war effort, and far removed from any front-line action.

Bill Nagle (2/1st Infantry Battalion) was captured on Crete in 1941. After a period endured at a filthy, verminous transit camp in Salonika, Greece, he was transported by cattle truck to Germany. As an NCO he was eligible under the rules of war for work parties, and during his stint in two Polish mines he experienced moments of great anxiety and terror. The first incident occurred in a coal mine near Cracow.

Bill Nagle's introduction to coal mining was at the beginning of winter, and the clothes allotted to him for this purpose were a coat and trousers of a heavy cotton material. He quickly found them too hot to wear on the coal face, so like his fellow prisoners he fashioned a form of G-string to wear, his being a sock turned into two thicknesses and held in place with fuse wire. When it was time to go up after a shift the men had to wait at the bottom of the shaft for the guards to come and get them. That was cold enough, but when they reached the top of the vertical shaft in the snow, the temperature may have plummeted to as low as 30 degrees below zero.

He had only been on the job for a few months when a cave-in occurred and he and five Poles were trapped for three days before being dug out. The trapped men had no timber to help from their end, so it was just a case of wait and hope for the best. The senior Pole took charge and the men all pooled their carbide, which they used in just one lamp for short spells at a time. When the rescue party broke through they passed in bowls of good hot vegetable soup, the best Nagle says he had tasted in years.

Periodically the prisoners were subjected to searches and these took place at odd times, such as two or three o'clock in the morning, by either Gestapo or SS Storm Troopers. During one of these searches the prisoners were bundled out into the snow while the SS tore their hut apart, looking for contraband or escape equipment. As the Germans looked around, one of the men outside noticed a searcher take a cake of soap from a shelf (soap then was worth its weight in gold) and slip it into his pocket. The camp leader was quickly informed, and he in turn told the German *Kommandant*; the *Kommandant* then passed this information along to the SS officer in charge. One thing the Germans would not tolerate was pilfering among soldiers. When the searchers finally came out, the man was pointed out to the waiting SS officer. The guilty culprit was ordered to empty out his pockets, disclosing the evidence of the cake of soap. Then came summary justice at its best—the man was stripped of his side arms and marched away forthwith. The camp *Kommandant* said the soldier's next stop would be the Russian Front. He was full of apologies for this incident, and said it was a good thing his own guards had seen what happened as it would serve as a warning to them.

Some time afterwards Bill Nagle and several others were moved to another mine, farther north on the outskirts of Warsaw. Here the temperature dropped down to 40 degrees below zero in winter. This was a gas mine and the men were issued with electric lamps, of which there were three types. The lowly worker had a lamp which cast an all-round glow; the overseers had a lamp which could detect gas, and all the big brass had a large lamp which had a very strong torch-like beam. Bill Nagle was to have three real spots of bother in this mine, each progressively worse.

The first piece of trouble he got into occurred on one night shift. He was doing repair work and pushing a skip full of rubbish along a shaft, when it suddenly became stuck. The continual pressure of the earth down below the surface could cause a good shaft one day to become impassable the next. This is what happened here; the side timber had squeezed inwards and impeded his progress. As he hunched down to try and force the skip through, an invisible pocket of gas passed down the shaft without warning and the Australian simply passed out. He fell down with his head to the side of the rails, missing the water which was between them, and in which he may well have drowned. Fortunately Nagle was found and carted out on a stretcher, but he still had to front up for work the following day.

Later on, still on night shift, he was dragging timber further along a shaft to drop it down to men below him in another shaft. He left his coat and trousers at the top of this shaft with his bread ration (kept in a small tin to stop the rats from getting it) in the pocket of his coat. He had just hooked onto a piece of timber with a wire-pulling apparatus when his lamp fizzled out and all he could do was sit down in the darkness until someone came to find out what had happened. Soon after he noticed a faint light down the end of the tunnel, and knowing the tunnel well by now he picked up his lamp and very, very slowly made his way towards the light.

It took a while as he inched along the tunnel, and by the time he got close enough to make out the owner of the lamp Nagle could see it was one of those known as the 'big brass'. Several of these men were half-Polish, half-German, and they were all despised by the regular Polish miners. Hearing the prisoner approaching along the tunnel the fellow turned, and Nagle could see the man was eating his ration of bread. 'You bastard', the enraged Australian cried, 'that's my bread you're eating!' The guard's only reaction was to laugh, enraging Nagle to the point where something had to happen—and did. He lashed out with a bunched first, and the shocked guard fell backwards both from the blow and the surprise of the sudden attack. Unfortunately for the man he had been sitting beside a 30-metre deep shaft, and as he fell he cried out in horror, before tumbling down the shaft where Nagle had earlier dropped his timber.

The shock hit the Australian as well; he knew it was unlikely the brute had survived the fall, and together with the realisation that he had actually killed another human being came the thought that he was in really big trouble. But as he stood there his Australian monkey cunning came to his rescue. As luck would have it, this particular guard had been using a lamp almost identical to Nagle's so he threw his now-defunct lamp down after the dead guard, picked up the man's good one, and made his way back along the tunnel to his timber where he waited for nearly fifteen minutes. Nagle recalled:

Living under those circumstances we nearly all learnt how to think and act like criminals. I dragged my timber to the top of the shaft, looked down, and saw a lot of lights. I yelled out as usual 'Under below!', and someone called out to hold everything as someone had fallen down the shaft. I climbed down to see what was happening, and what do you know—one of the big brass had been too sneaky, had fallen down and broken his silly neck. It was put down as an accident caused by a deficient lamp. My legs were trembling so much it took me a long time to climb back up the shaft. I felt like laughing and crying at the same time.

Bill Nagle's next bout of bother occurred when he was working on the face with his two English mates, both from the Royal Tank Corps. Too much coal had been blown, and when the Poles knocked off, the three prisoners were told to stay behind; their job would be to get rid of the coal left behind before the powder monkeys came along to blow some more coal for the next shift. It was one particularly nasty guard, again a half-German, half-Polish fellow, who had demanded that the prisoners remain behind, and he was as keen to see the work done as the prisoners were to finish up and get out of the mine. Heated words were exchanged; tempers flared, and the situation became extremely volatile.

The guard seemed to realise that he was losing the verbal argument against three hostile prisoners, and made the mistake of going for his gun. The next few moments, as Nagle recalls, were dramatic.

A natural instinct for survival came to the fore and I swung my shovel, catching him across the neck, nearly severing his head from his shoulders. He was dead before he hit the ground. This meant a firing squad for sure this time if we were caught, so we buried him in the sand behind us, washed away the blood, and had the good sense to take his lamp with us. We droppd this off at the lamp room on the way out. To all intents and purposes he had come up from below, and was never seen again.

Bill Nagle managed to survive the war and returned to Australia. Today he remembers his sojourn in the Polish mines with a mixture of sadness and bitterness, but through it all the finest memory he has is of the loyalty and staunchness of his British mates, who endured those months of terror with him.

Another Australian sent to work in the mines was Victorian Jim Shaw (2/2nd Field Regiment). Having made his first unsuccessful escape from a work camp near the Swiss–Italian border in 1942, he was given 21 days in the cells, then sent to a special *Strafelager* (punishment camp) for escapers.

This camp was an open-cut mine, near a small village named Gross Veitch, where the prisoners dug for a mineral called magnesite. Jim Shaw was placed in the punishment cells, or bunkers, a number of times for not doing sufficient work. After an argument with a civilian he was sentenced to ten days' solitary confinement for attempted assault.

A Queenslander known as 'Scotty' was the camp's Man of Confidence. Each POW camp had such a person, responsible for liaising with the German *Kommandant* on matters pertaining to the prisoners' well-being. Scotty's first reaction to Jim Shaw's forthcoming imprisonment was to call the prisoners out on strike! This however was settled quite quickly the next morning by the guards when they surrounded the barracks, then entered, and commenced firing through the roof. When none of the prisoners moved, one Englishman was shot through the hip on his bed. Naturally this ended the strike; Shaw was thrown into the bunker, and later marched into a gaol in the base of the Town Hall at Klein Veitch, where he spent his ten days on a sparse diet of cabbage soup and potatoes twice daily. The first few evenings in the gaol Jim Shaw was visited by the village idiot, who used to come to the small barred window on ground level and poke faces at the prisoner, and so Jim decided to put a stop to that.

I grew quite tired of this, and one evening I took the toilet bucket and threw the contents all over him! I didn't see him again. After doing my ten days I was returned to the work camp, and was there for another twelve months. I would have to say that the cooperation between us prisoners was the best I have ever experienced. The mateship was terrific.

3

Revenge

CORPORAL George Thompson, from the 2/2nd Field Ambulance, was captured by German paratroopers in the Corinth Canal on Anzac Day, 1941. Sent to Stalag VIIIB, Lamsdorf, he experienced both the best and worst in his fellow prisoners. One vivid memory he had concerns the discovery of a German spy in their midst.

It was noticed that one particular inmate seemed to be asking a lot of questions, and moved from compound to compound with ease, still asking questions. So a group of POWs grabbed him one night and he finally admitted to being a German intelligence officer; he had his papers, his rank number and visa on him, so the game was up. Ten NCOs, including Thompson, held a clandestine trial to determine the spy's fate. 'Guilty was the verdict. We then drew cards to knock him off—no one knew who had the card, only the holder. This man did his duty, then [the body] was disposed of by all ten members—well and truly buried and never found.'

After a couple of days the Germans began to miss their agent, and search parties became larger and more frequent. When he didn't turn up the Germans knew that foul play had occurred, and marched every inmate out of the camp and onto some farm land located at one side of the camp. It was cold, and it snowed frequently, but the prisoners were made to stand their ground, encircled by 500 troops with guard dogs, for two days and nights.

Finally the Germans gave up and the prisoners were allowed back into the camp, which had been torn apart by security troops and guards. Sniffer dogs had been unable to find any trace of the missing agent. Although many of the prisoners could guess the reason for the massive search, George Thompson says: 'The only people who knew what it was all about were the ten previously mentioned'.

Within Lamsdorf was an area known as the Glasgow Compound, where a vicious band of nearly 150 Scottish thugs terrorised the other inmates with acts of brutality and sadism; they beat and slashed with cut-throat razors those who challenged them, with apparent impunity. This unsavoury mob of hooligans was led by Duke Boyle, who lorded over his Razor Gang (as they were known) with the full knowledge of the Germans. Boyle and his gang, assigned cushy jobs in the cookhouse, worked every racket imaginable with corrupt guards, stole food and cigarettes from Red Cross parcels and ran a vast black-market enterprise. Stan Wick (2/2nd Bn) wrote this of Boyle:

> There were other racketeers in Stalag VIIIB but the most fearsome was Duke Boyle, who had been a gang leader in Glasgow and who carried a cut-throat razor in his top outside pocket, the blade being opened up and firmly bound for instant use. He ruled his empire with an iron hand and his power was known to the German guards. He seemed to come and go out of camp as he pleased and would re-appear mysteriously after an absence of some days. He had once made a clean getaway, but had been picked up by the Gestapo and placed in solitary confinement, but even there he lived well and issued his orders. When word was passed on that 'The Duke says . . .', it was unwise to disobey. Incidentally, stealing was extremely rare in this cut-throat world. You would either be dumped in the cesspit under the latrines or get a knife in your back that night.

As they were comparatively well-fed and pampered, several of the Glaswegians extended their activities to include rape. George Thompson recalls the time that two young inmates were placed into the Glasgow Compound to tend to the demands of this evil and hated group.

A fresh-faced English lad and his mate, who had come from a working party, were made to join others who swept the floors and even washed the clothing of the hut's leaders, about ten stand-over men. Not long after the two young men were gang raped by this mob. Neither of these poor lads was homosexual, so it was in shame and dread they told some other prisoners they feared for their lives.

By now those prisoners also knew that cigarettes, chocolates and other food items sent to them by the Red Cross were disappearing. Every compound had complaints of thieving, and all the skull duggery could be traced back to the Glasgow Compound. Then one day another young Australian lad was picked on by two Glaswegians. He dropped one with a mighty blow, but the other no-hoper slashed him across the face with a razor blade. The next day, as a result, the men gathered together an attacking party of Aussies, New Zealanders and Canadians. Some had knuckle dusters made from tin, while the rest had stones and other harmful assault items. Thompson's group was led by Sergeant Alan Sneddon (eldest brother of the late Sir Billy) and Dave Harris from Western Australia—the fellow who had been cut.

The outraged group swept into the Glasgow Compound and confronted the ring leaders, whom they managed to separate from the rest. After 'knocking a few heads' as George Thompson described the ensuing battle, and issuing stern threats to the leaders, they retired to their own compound. Results came quickly; the Glasgow Compound gang was moved out of the camp within four days, and the other inmates received a 50 per cent increase in their food rations. 'So ended rape to our knowledge', was Thompson's closing remark on the subject.

4

Only the stars to guide

I N May 1942 there was a mass tunnel escape from Stalag IIIE at Dobrilugk–Kirchain. Although the camp was only 150 metres square, housing some 200 NCO prisoners of war, there was one guard for every two prisoners. The men, from the British, Canadian, Australian and New Zealand air forces, together with some from the Fleet Air Arm, had been transferred to Stalag IIIE when the camps at Lamsdorf and Sagan became overcrowded.

It was a classic tunnel escape; a wide shaft was dug down to a depth of two metres below No. 2 barrack, and the tunnel, shored with bed boards, was driven out some 70 metres. On the evening of 11 May the end of the tunnel was breached and 52 men managed to make their escape before dawn. When the German Army guards finally realised the extent of the escape a massive search was organised within a 160-kilometre radius of the camp. Details of the escape were broadcast; the Hitler Youth and Home Guards combined with troops and aircraft to run the men down. Some were recaptured quickly and all were rounded up within ten days. One barefoot Canadian, his hands held high in surrender, was shot dead by an overanxious policeman when he pointed to his feet, requesting permission to put on his boots.

By coincidence, the same number of POWs escaped from a similar tunnel the following year at Arbeitskommando 865,

Molsdorf—a camp attached to Stalag IXC, Bad Sulza. Flight Sergeant Jack Garland was the sole Australian involved in this particular escape.

Garland, from 97 Squadron, was a Lancaster mid-upper gunner whose aircraft was shot down during a raid on Kassell on the night of 27–28 August 1942. He and Flight Engineer Fred Ambrose, an Australian in the RAF, were the only survivors from their crew. After receiving attention in a Reserve hospital at Duisberg for a broken femur and shrapnel wounds sustained in getting out of the doomed aircraft, Garland was transferred to a hospital at Dulag Luft, where he was interrogated in his bed and then taken to Obermassfeld hospital, which was attached to Stalag IXC and was nominated as Arbeitskommando 1249. When the airman was sufficiently recovered he was transferred to another Arbeitskommando attached to Stalag IXC, number 865.

This camp, in Thuringia, was situated on a flat area of ground two kilometres east of the village of Molsdorf. Designed to hold between three and four hundred prisoners, the camp consisted of a large group of huts surrounded by a three-metre high, double-apron barbed-wire fence. A sentry box stood at the main southern gates and two sentry towers, complete with machine-guns and searchlights, were situated at diagonal corners of the camp. Guards patrolled the perimeter with Alsatian dogs, while others roamed the compound. Molsdorf was basically a transit camp populated by prisoners going to and from hospital, or from one work place to another, and as such the guards' discipline and watchfulness was not of the highest calibre.

Garland soon discovered that a tunnel had been started and was being built by a group of British engineers in the camp who had been captured at Dunkirk and St Valery. After making some furtive enquiries he was invited to join their effort in exchange for a little work on the project; his escape partner was to be a large lump of a man named Jack Lawrence, a huge sailor who hailed from Bristol.

The tunnel took about six weeks to construct, and the exit

was about halfway up the side of a stormwater canal to the west of the camp, about two metres above water level. There was very little in the way of security in the camp and the night of the escape all those who were going gradually made their way to Garland's room. It was a tense time for everyone as they waited for the designated hour. The bunk which hid the shaft was moved to one side and the hole exposed; a couple of engineers went down the tunnel and started work on the final breach into the stormwater canal. A strict watch was kept in the *Lager*, although not too many guards would venture outside their barracks at night except those in the towers and the ones detailed to patrol the outside of the camp.

It was growing hot and uncomfortable in the room when the first group was told to start making their way into the shaft. Being the senior NCO in the camp who was going to venture on the outside, the soldiers had asked Jack Garland to lead the bunch out. He feels now it was a bit of a con job.

I think the English fellows had worked it out beforehand that if there was to be any sort of trouble on exiting the camp the Australian could carry the can!

The idea was for us to go out in parties of twelve. It was pitch black in the tunnel, and there was no moon as we emerged into the fresh air. We more or less fell into the canal, waiting till all of our group were in the canal before moving off, but had only gone a few metres when one of the tower guards swung his searchlight down the canal, bathing us in the harsh light. It was as well we had been hugging the sides of the rough-hewn ditch as we all merged into the edge and he was unable to see us. Luckily nothing happened, the light moved on, and we scrambled to the far end of the camp. We peeped over the rim of the canal and could see the patrolling guard disappearing towards the *Vorlager*, so we quickly ran the forty or so metres to the cover of the woods where our hearts resumed their normal rhythm.

With only the stars to guide them, Garland and Lawrence made their way towards the railhead at Eisenach, blundering at one time into an ice-cold stream, unseen in the darkness. Shortly after they observed a flickering light approaching and froze in their tracks, but to their relief it turned out to be nothing more than a firefly. As dawn was breaking on that morning, 25 March 1943, the two men clambered into a ditch running behind a small village and covered themselves with straw to await the cover of night. Farmers came to work nearby, and they spent several uncomfortable hours watching them in the fields. At four o'clock in the afternoon a youth aged about eleven, apparently on his way home from school, came tramping up the ditch and trod on Garland's concealed leg. The lad screamed with fright and the farm workers came running over to see what the trouble was. Garland and Lawrence reluctantly emerged from beneath the straw and were soon in the custody of a fat policeman brandishing an outsized revolver. He marched them off to the local village and with no suitably secure place to leave them, the fellow innocently locked his prisoners in the cellar of the *Gasthaus* for the night. This was quite a mistake on his part.

In the morning when he came to pick them up, the policeman was greeted by an unexpected situation. His two prisoners had liberally sampled the contents of most of the bottles in the cellar, and were in a very happy state of mind. Nevertheless, the enraged policeman had orders to march his intoxicated charges back to the camp, all the time shouting to the field workers that he had captured some particularly dangerous enemy airmen.

Some of these workers were Serbian prisoners, and as the prisoners passed they respectfully came to attention, saluted and cheered. This did not impress the fat policeman, who'd had about enough for the day. He pulled out his revolver, fired a couple of bullets over their heads, and shouted abuse that didn't seem to concern the Serbs one little bit.

In all, 52 men escaped from the camp, and although they were quickly recaptured, one managed to elude the patrols and reached freedom in Switzerland. The *Kommandant* and some of his guards were removed, presumably to do penance on the Eastern Front, while Jack Garland was sentenced to three months'

road labour for his part in the escape, in contravention of the
Geneva Convention rules regarding recaptured prisoners.

Ten days after the escape I was taken to a small village to do our
hard labour; an old *Feldwebel* was in charge and he set us to digging
up a section of road. We would just lift the picks and let them drop
to the roadway. The *Feldwebel* did his crumpet and after screaming
'*Nein, Nein, Nein!*' lifted a pick and demonstrated the correct method
of road digging. He managed to do in five minutes the same amount
of work that had taken us all of the morning!

5

Airmen on the run

I N all, 41 Australian airmen successfully escaped from German prisoner of war camps, but only five eventually made it back to England through neutral territory.

Several RAAF prisoners changed identities with enlisted men from working camps, where escape was immeasurably easier. Nineteen Australians escaped in this manner, principally from camps located at Lamsdorf and Muhlberg. Three of the total eleven air force prisoners who made it back to England or the Allied lines from Lamsdorf were Australians.

Warrant Officers K.B. Chisholm and W.G. Reed, on separate occasions, exchanged places with British Army privates and were sent on working parties, from which they absconded. Chisholm (No. 452 Squadron) teamed up with two Dutch escapers in Warsaw after his escape from a work camp near Gleiwitz on 11 August 1942. The three men made their way to Paris, where they managed to stay in hiding until the liberation of the French capital. Chisholm was returned to England.

Bill Reed, from No. 460 Squadron, had already escaped three times and had twice been recaptured after making it onto Swedish ships, but his determination to escape was resolute. Not long after D-Day, Reed told his fellow crew member David Radke, 'I'm going to see the Front from the other side!'

Impressed perhaps by Bill Reed's efforts, another of his crew, observer Max Wyllie, decided to attempt a similar change of identity ruse, and teamed up with Derek Scott from Tenterfield, New South Wales—a fighter pilot from No. 3 Squadron. Scott was another determined escaper who, having been taken by the Germans when he was shot down, escaped and evaded capture for six months in Greece.

Max Wyllie was from Queensland, a large, affable personality whose good nature and caring concern for his fellow man endeared the former New Farm (Brisbane) Rugby player to those who came in contact with him. Wyllie, the observer, and Reed, rear gunner, had managed to bale out of their blazing Wellington Mk IV after being hit following an attack on Bremen on the night of 2–3 July 1942. Together with wireless operator David Radke, they were the only survivors of the six-man, all-Australian crew. Front gunner Bill Taylor managed to parachute clear of the doomed aircraft but hit high tension wires near the ground and was electrocuted. The skipper, Max Johnson, died in the cockpit, while second pilot Darryl Dowling left it too late to bale out, jumping only seconds before impact. The three survivors were rounded up at Rheine, near the Dutch border, and after the usual interrogation at Dulag Luft were transferred to Lamsdorf on 22 July 1942.

Wyllie and Scott exchanged places with two Palestinian Jews, and under their assumed names left Lamsdorf early in April the following year. In the meantime David Radke had taken one of the Jewish workers, Alex Palenker, into their hut under Max's name. But the escape attempt had a tragic conclusion.

About 23 April the camp guards burst into the hut, seized Palenker and thrust him into the camp 'cooler' together with the other substitute. The Senior British Officer, R.S.M. Sheriff, was informed that Derek Scott was already in the cooler, and that his escaping partner, Wyllie, had been shot and killed, and was buried at a place called Kressendorf, near the Polish border. Having served his 21 days for escaping, Derek Scott was released from his cell in early May and filled in many of the facts of the tragic incident for David Radke.

Scotty and Wyllie had managed to slip away from their working party and had been on the loose for two or three days. Despite timetables for trains and identity papers they just couldn't get the break required to catch a train north to the Baltic via Breslau. Radke believes the two men had found themselves in the Gleiwitz–Kattowitz area, and following the first big German reverses on the Russian Front the trains were continually full of wounded returning from, or reinforcements going to, the east. April was still cold and they were desperately looking for some shelter as they trudged along the rail line. Around 2.00 a.m. on the 21st or 22nd they saw a little railway station in the distance, and as it was cold, dark and foggy they decided to make for it. They were aware that some stations were patrolled, but felt that this one was small and, if guarded, they would be able to give themselves up if confronted.

Just as they neared the siding a young guard jumped out in front of them with his rifle aimed low at Max's midriff, shouting excitedly. As Max tried to explain that they were 'Englander Kriegsgefangener' and was feeling round his neck for his camp registration disc, the guard shot him from point blank range, hitting Max in the stomach. Max's hand went to his stomach, and as he collapsed slowly, turning away from the guard, another bullet entered his back.

The first shot had awakened people in some small nearby houses, and they were running out to the scene of the commotion when the guard fired the second shot. In a real panic the guard screamed at Derek Scott to run—obviously a shot in the back of the other 'escaping prisoner' would be a good excuse for his actions. But Scott stood his ground as the startled older men arrived in nightware and coats. They remonstrated with the panicky guard, and one went to telephone for some more soldiers, but their quick arrival on the scene had undoubtedly saved Scott's life. Some soldiers duly turned up, taking custody of Derek Scott, and the body of Max Wyllie.

David Radke is still saddened by the lack of any subsequent action.

Despite complaints to the Swiss Protecting Authority, I am unaware of any final action over Max's death from April 1943 up to the latter part of 1944 when the SS took over our camp. Rumour had it that the guard was found guilty of some breach of military discipline and 'suitably punished', whatever that may mean. Max's death affected a lot of people in many ways in VIIIB as he was such a popular, well-known figure. I decided to put off my own plans for an escape, but his death made Bill Reed all the more determined to get away.

Saddened, but undeterred by the tragedy, Bill Reed once again exchanged identities with a British Army private and was sent as part of a working party to a coal mine at Beuthen. Together with a German-speaking private, Reed slipped away from the mine on 11 July and walked into Beuthen. From here they travelled by tram and train to Breslau.

During this time their forged documents were examined, but stood up well to scrutiny. From Breslau they travelled by train to Kustrin via Frankfurt-on-Oder and then journeyed on to Stettin. At suburban Gotzlow they managed to clamber around a wharf fence and to hide aboard a Swedish ship, where they were helped by an English-speaking Swedish engineer. They survived a German search of the vessel before it sailed, and surrendered themselves to the Swedish police once the ship docked at Solvesborg, from where they were taken to Stockholm. Here they reported to the British Legation.

Reed was later flown back to England in the bomb bay of a Mosquito, and was awarded the Distinguished Conduct Medal in recognition of his four escape attempts. Bill Reed returned home to Australia, but died in a road accident on 20 January 1954.

6

Life and death under the Italians

OF all military reversals suffered by British and Allied forces during the war, few caused greater shock than the sudden and unexpected loss of the former Italian fortress at Tobruk.

At the same time as the campaigns in Greece and Crete were being fought, the forces of the German desert commander, Erwin Rommel, had overwhelmed those of General Wavell in Cyrenaica, driving them relentlessly back into Egypt. But at Tobruk the Allies mounted a stand, managing to repulse and effectively tie up the Axis army for eight crucial months.

Tobruk, its harbour nestling in the Mediterranean Sea, lay 100 kilometres west of the Egyptian frontier in Cyrenaica, the eastern province of Libya. Allied forces, including the Australian 9th Division, continually thwarted and repelled Rommel's attempts to acquire Tobruk Harbour, effectively preventing the brilliant German strategist from concentrating his panzer units for the planned push to the Nile Delta.

But Rommel, under extreme pressure from Hitler, mounted a huge assault in mid-1942. This time his units overwhelmed the slender garrison forces. Early on the morning of 21 June a white flag was raised over Tobruk; over 30 000 men and a vast amount of armaments, vehicles and supplies fell into enemy hands. A valiant and defiant defence was at an end.

The temporary prison camp for the captives taken at Tobruk

stood atop an escarpment overlooking the ancient city. The highest area of the escarpment was comparatively flat, stretching back as a plateau right along the coast and deep inland. Being quite high and close to the sea it was naturally exposed to the elements; at the time of the fall of Tobruk the last of the *khamseens* (sandstorms) was covering everything in its path with suffocatingly fine dust and sand. On the exposed plateau, and near the remains of a fire-gutted NAAFI store, a POW 'cage' had been hastily erected by the simple expedient of laying down a vast circle of coiled Danert barbed wire. A narrow gap serving as an entrance had been left, through which the prisoners could pass inside, and all round the wire heavily armed guards were positioned with machine-guns at the ready for any signs of escape or insurrection.

If the sombre journey up to this temporary prison pen had been depressing for the new prisoners, the actual sight of the cage was nothing short of dismaying. A vast congregation of ill-clad, sorry-looking humanity was huddled together in clusters for shelter, or simply standing looking balefully out through the wire. There were close on 27 000 men in the cage, and this mass of miserable captives seemed to extend as far as the eye could see in every direction.

With the exception of two small tents which were being used as sick rooms by the medical staff, there was absolutely no shelter from the swirling wind and stinging desert sand. Most of the men who had been there for several days presented a pitiful sight; their clothes, hair and faces were encrusted with sand.

The prisoners were assembled in ragged groups according to their units, but some who had been captured alone simply squatted by themselves in dejection, talking to no one and with little inclination to find anyone they knew. Sun-dried, grimy faces were pinched and drawn, with a look of blank hopelessness and apathy that one would generally not see outside of war. The men were provided with food just once a day, and this took the form of a tin of bully beef to be shared between four, two rock-hard army biscuits, and a cup of warm, brackish water per person. Eventually convoys of lorries began arriving to evacuate the cage, and the prisoners were transported towards Derna.

Gunner Horace Redding from South Australia wrote in his diary:

> We left Tobruk on the 29th of June in trucks of one hundred men ... The first day brought us to Timini, where we just laid about on a swampy field. Those hundreds of prisoners who'd been here before us had left their empty tins, excreta and urine anywhere on the swampy ground. No hygiene—the air was stinking. Those hard biscuits were replaced by a loaf of bread; the size was about a quarter of those at home. It was heaven to chew it after the days on those biscuits. Some actually burnt their bread and biscuits to make coffee.

At Derna the prisoners were crammed into an old stone fort built on top of a slight rise. The unlucky ones who could not find accommodation in the fort were herded off into the high-walled grounds of a nearby graveyard. Conditions here were marginally better, although the men were now able to observe first hand the barbarous attitude of the Axis powers.

The root of the evil at Derna was the prison commandant, a short, fat Italian captain, who stamped and screamed hysterically, and whose invective was not only directed at the prisoners, but at his own men, whom he berated loudly and vigorously. It was quite common at this stage of the war for British POWs to be on the receiving end of some particularly harsh treatment by the Italians who, in light of the vast numbers of their countrymen held prisoner by the British, took unwarranted delight in having their own captive enemy troops to bully and push around. One day two men quite innocently ventured too close to the wire surrounding the fort; without any warning they were shot dead by a sentry and their bodies, on the direct orders of the commandant, left as they fell for 24 hours. New prisoners were thus warned of the dire punishment awaiting all who disobeyed Italian orders.

Accommodation in the fort was severely limited. As many of

the prisoners as could be packed into the rooms were marched in and the doors locked, the others being forced to lie down on the cobbled courtyard outside. As can be imagined, the floor space available for lying down in the rooms was somewhat limited, and the men complained derisively about being treated like sardines. Soon after their arrival a long-overdue ration of Italian bully beef and biscuit was dispensed to all, and a quantity of fresh water measured out. Most of the prisoners had managed to retain their knives to this time, but one of the first things the guards did as soon as the men were brought in was to confiscate such things as knives, forks, scissors, razors (and in some cases, watches) at the point of a bayonet. When the prisoners protested that they would be unable to open the tins of bully beef without their knives, they were instructed to kick them open with their boots!

Any sanitary arrangements which might have once existed were now totally useless; the latrines had long since become choked up and little or no attempt had been made to clear them. As one diarist recorded: 'they resembled so many manure heaps and were the breeding places for swarms of maggots and flies. The very serious outbreak of dysentry [sic] which developed soon after this was, I am certain, directly attributable to this awful place.'

Conditions similar to these were experienced by rapidly growing numbers of prisoners in other camps at Barce and Benghazi. Suffering from exposure and lack of proper nourishment, the men's resistance to disease, particularly dysentery, was considerably lowered. The sudden and protracted lack of vitamins meant that any bodily wounds, however minor, quickly developed into chronic ulcers and only healed, albeit slowly, with proper medical attention.

German transport planes carried some of the overflow of prisoners from Barce into Italy. For the majority, however, they had to stay put in the filthy, disease-ridden desert camps. The Italians were unable to ship their prisoners across the Mediterranean for some time due to the British naval blockade, so auxiliary camps were set up a thousand kilometres to the west in Tripolitania. There, recently captured prisoners joined thousands of other weary troops, taken prior to the fall of Tobruk.

Food supplies, inadequate as they were to prevent severe malnutrition, were cut even further by unscrupulous Italian quartermasters, who maintained a flourishing food trade with the Arabs, and ate royally while prisoners died of starvation and related diseases. Complaints to indifferent camp commandants were for the most part ignored.

Casualties in the Tripolitanian camps were not shipped to Italy until late November, by which time the prisoners were gaunt, starving and diseased.

Garvan ('Snowy') Drew, of the 2/15th Australian Infantry Battalion, was one of those thousands held in a German working camp in Tripoli, one known officially as Feldpost 12545. The camp, he recalls, had previously been an institution for the training of Italian cadets. He continues:

The camp was a miserable enclosure about fifty metres by twelve metres, flanked by five stone barracks, a cookhouse, and a wooden hut with a high wall at one end. Along the northern side of the camp ran a footway and a low row of taps and wash basins, with a toilet at the end of the pathway. It was actually two toilets back to back, and was built in the traditional Italian style where one squatted down over a hole in the floor. Beyond the pathway was a narrow beach and the sea, which was enclosed by barbed wire about twenty metres out. This camp housed about three hundred prisoners, mostly Australian and English taken in Rommel's advance through Libya.

The German *Kommandant* of the camp, whom the men referred to as 'Battle Axe' was *Oberleutnant* Held, who proved to be a ruthless and vindictive man who never failed to show his hatred of the British. He would come on parade clearly affected by liquor, shouting and raving.

The prisoners were split into groups of about fifty and worked at the supply dumps concealed in the bush-covered hills around Tripoli. Down at the docks they unloaded ammunition from the ships, while at other dumps known as 'Aero' and 'Kilos 5, 6 and 8' they loaded bombs of 200, 500 and 1000 pounds. At the petrol dumps they handled 44-gallon drums of fuel in addition to the well-known Jerry cans. All of which of course was contrary to the rules of the Geneva Convention.

Snowy Drew's day would start about 4.00 a.m. when the working party arose. Breakfast consisted of a cup of coffee, which was made of burnt wheat or barley, a couple of slices of *Dauerbrat*, which was an unpalatable type of black sliced bread, and a cubic inch of jam. At times the men arrived back at night at eleven o'clock to an evening meal of a ladle of stew. This would often be eaten in total darkness as the British continuously bombed Tripoli by night, so all would be blacked out.

One night the bombing was particularly heavy. Bombs were dropped on Italian barracks directly across the road, and the windows and doors in the POW camp were blown in. In the midst of this raid, with pieces of flak falling in the compound, the prisoners were called out on parade. The *Kommandant*, mad with liquor and rage, wanted to know who had broken in the doors of the storeroom and cookhouse! No one could convince him that the bombs had been the culprits, but after an hour of shouting and waving his anger abated and the men were allowed to return to their beds.

Sabotage was practised as much as possible. Working at the docks presented Drew and his mates with the opportunity to drop an occasional shell or two into the sea. Similarly, working at petrol dumps, they found it relatively easy to feed a few handfuls of sand into the Jerry cans of petrol and oil, and to loosen the bungs on several 44-gallon drums. 'Our clothes were always washed in petrol', Drew remembers with amusement, 'taking four gallons to wash a shirt and eight to wash a pair of trousers! As well as cleaning our clothes the petrol also got rid of the body lice.'

The one place that none of the prisoners minded working in were the food stores at a place appropriately named 'Fatma', which was a large rectangle of supply sheds. Some of these sheds contained ammunition, but the main one was a food store where the Italians unloaded trucks and stacked cases of various foods, which would have been the plunder of Europe. Norwegian sardines, Danish butter, French wines, Italian jams and fruits, as well as cases of German emergency ration chocolate— all were considered fair game and devoured eagerly by the hungry prisoners. When rostered to work in these stores the men certainly ate well; they had the pick of the store. Every man carried a small opener made from the hoop iron which was used to bind the cases. Naturally they were caught at times and the punishment was usually ten days' solitary confinement in a small cell. Needless to say, there was always a long waiting list for confinement!

One day Snowy Drew was caught with a can of peaches which he had just opened, and was so intent on eating them he didn't hear the German guard approaching. The outraged guard ranted and raved as all Germans seemed to do. Drew unwisely replied with 'Shut up, you German bastard!' With hindsight it was a silly thing for him to have done, but at the time it seemed appropriate. They took him back to camp where he was paraded before the *Kommandant* (who also ranted and raved) and assured Drew of the legitimacy of all German soldiers. He was then taken to a small room by two German NCOs who proceeded to give him a severe beating with their fists, as well as using their boots and belting him across the head with their pistols. One of the guards then levelled his pistol at Drew's forehead.

I thought, this is it, this is the finish. I shut my eyes and in that moment I said goodbye to all my family. I opened my eyes after a while and he was lowering the pistol. I was then given twenty-one days' solitary confinement, and on completion told that if I was a good boy I could stay in Tripoli, or I would be sent to Italy. I chose Italy.

After that episode prisoners no longer worked at the 'Fatma'. They employed the natives instead. But knowing what thieves the Arabs were, I am sure their losses would have been greater!

7

The luck of the draw

T HE difference between life and death can sometimes fall to chance or, as John Frizell (2/3rd Anti-Tank Regiment and 2/28th Battalion, 9th Division) puts it—'the luck of the draw'.

Following the fall of Tobruk in June 1942 the British Eighth Army fell back in disarray to a small place on the railway line and coast road called El Alamein, just 110 kilometres west of Alexandria.

An epic and historic battle was to be waged at El Alamein in late October 1942, but this story relates mainly to events following a less publicised but equally bitter and bloody struggle along the low El Alamein ridges during the month of July; an engagement now called the 'First Battle of Alamein'—a battle which stopped Erwin Rommel in his tracks and saved the Nile Delta.

Up in Syria and Lebanon the Australian 9th Division, while digging fortifications and manoeuvring around the northern borders in anticipation of a possible German thrust through Turkey, was also thinking it was packing its bags in readiness for a return to Australia to fight the Japanese. The Kiwis were still up in the Western Desert, also thinking of the threat in the Pacific.

So much for expectations—Rommel broke out of his lair and by 6 June had smashed the British lines and taken 4000 prisoners. By 21 June, when the Australian 9th Division was on manoeuvres up in the Fourgloss Desert in the Turkish border area, Tobruk fell with hardly a shot being fired by its then main defenders, the South Africans. This disaster dismayed and disgusted the 9th Division, as many of its elements had held Tobruk for seven months in 1941. The Australians' ticket home started to look frayed around the edges, although the optimists kept on saying 'They wouldn't send us back up the desert—they need us at home.'

Sure enough, after moving out of Lebanon by rail and road, as part of a deception plan, the division travelled a devious route through Homs, Baalbek, Rayek and Damascus, then through Tiberias and Haifa and across the desert to the Suez Canal. Here, it turned right and not left, and headed for the Nile Delta, leaving the *Queen Mary* swinging on her anchor at Port Tewfiq.

On the way through Cairo and Alexandria the bemused men were all told 'not to look like Australians'—a bit difficult! At one stage though someone must have fallen for the gag, as it was learnt that the German agents had reported that the division moving up the line (moving well and truly against the traffic!) consisted, in fact, of South Africans dressed up as Aussies! Other locals however yelled out 'Hello Aussie, welcome back!' By this time even the optimists had given up and were now saying 'Well . . . it is about time we did a show with the Kiwis'. And so it was to be . . .

On 10 July the 26th Brigade opened the Australian action with an attack on the notorious Tel El Eisa Ridge (the Hill of Jesus as it came to be known). Between then and 27 July a series of savage battles raged across the low features of Tel El Eisa, Makh-khad and Miteiriya Ridges which lay between the coast and the impassable sand sea of the Qattara Depression.

During these battles, John Frizell was transferred from 2/3rd Anti-Tank Regiment to 2/28th Infantry Battalion, as a consequence of the reforming of the anti-tank companies which had been disbanded when the regiment took over the divisional anti-tank role late in 1941. This restructuring was necessary to try and counter the far superior German Mark 3 and Mark 4 tanks. And so he came to be engaged in the brilliantly executed but fateful attack by 2/28th Battalion on Miteiriya Ridge (or Ruin Ridge as the Allies called it) which took place on the night of 26 July in bright moonlight.

The 2/28th took the ridge, the major objective for both sides, with the promise of tank support next morning. This was the third time in a week that they had taken this ridge, having been mysteriously withdrawn on the two previous occasions. On this occasion they were ordered to hold on and they did, with heavy casualties against savage counterattacks until nearly midday on 27 July. The promised relief by armour was repulsed by the Germans early in the morning, with the loss of 22 British tanks. The 28th, plus a company of 2/2nd Machine Gunners, 12 Battery of 2/3rd Anti-Tank Regiment and support units, out of ammunition and exhausted, were forced to surrender. The Commanding Officer, Colonel L. McCarter, M.C., had no other option. The 28th was virtually destroyed, with only 92 men held in reserve when the action began.

Once 'in the bag' the Ruin Ridge survivors were sadly obliged to travel the long, hard and hungry road up the Western Desert, through El Daba, Hal-Faya Pass, Sollum, Tobruk and Derna until they reached Benghazi, to join thousands of Allied prisoners (Aussies, Kiwis, South Africans, English and Indians) held there awaiting transfer by sea to POW camps in Italy.

Conditions in the Benghazi 'cage' were harsh, with little food, water or medical attention. The men were hungry, ill-clad and suffering from dysentery, desert sores and unattended wounds. Thus, by 16 August, it came as almost a bitter relief to be told they would embark on two freighters, bound for Italy, with nearly 5000 prisoners crammed into the holds of either the *Franco Josi* or the *Nino Bixio*. As to which vessel each prisoner was to join, this became a matter of pure fate. They were lined up at tables where two Italian officers took their particulars and handed out red or blue 'boarding passes'. One colour denoted *Franco Josi* and the other colour the *Nino Bixio*—Frizell cannot recall which was which. In 'the luck of the draw' he was given a ticket for the *Franco Josi* and together with the other POWs was duly bundled on board and herded into the holds in appalling conditions. In company with the *Nino Bixio* and escorted by two Italian destroyers and a cruiser, they set out across the Mediterranean towards Taranto, in southern Italy.

At this point the story flashes back to a day in 1939 when a newly launched British submarine, HMS *Thetis*, left Birkenhead in England for diving trials, with 103 men on board. When the trials began, *Thetis* refused to dive; in trying to rectify the fault a watertight door jammed open and *Thetis* sank like a stone. Only four of the crew survived, using the Davis escape apparatus. The vessel was later salvaged, refurbished, and recommissioned as HMS *Thunderbolt*, following which she was sent off to the Mediterranean for active service. Subsequent records show that 'after a successful operation she disappeared in 1943'.

The 'successful operation' referred to is assumed to be that in which *Thunderbolt* sneaked up under two Italian freighters named *Franco Josi* and *Nino Bixio* at 1500 hours on 17 August 1942, in the vicinity of Crete, and fired two torpedoes. Little did her skipper know that his targets held about 5000 Allied prisoners trapped below decks. The two torpedoes narrowly missed the bow of the *Franco Josi* but found their mark in the engine room and number one hold of the *Nino Bixio*, which was steaming abreast of the more fortunate vessel. Frizell recalls:

> The two explosions which devastated *Nino Bixio* reverberated through our ship, causing understandable consternation among the prisoners crammed below, their guards and crew. Those of us below decks could only guess at what had happened. On deck, all was confusion, with a fair degree of panic among the Italian crew, which was soon brought under control by their officers and the small group of gentlemen from the Afrika Korps who were on board to make sure we all enjoyed our free Mediterranean cruise.

From the few prisoners who had been allowed on deck for latrine duties Frizell and the others soon learned that the *Nino Bixio* had been torpedoed and was listing badly. They considered the possibilities of their ship being smitten at any moment by more torpedoes, of their being dramatically liberated by the British Navy, and the option of charging up to the decks and taking over the ship. The first possibility appeared to be the more likely, but they hadn't thought of another possibility, which was that their ship and its three escort vessels would simply take off and leave the crippled ship to her fate. This sensible action (from the Italians' point of view) was taken, and the surviving freighter steamed off with its escort ships, which were in such a hurry to vacate the area that they had not dropped so much as a single depth charge by way of retaliation. The air escort had also departed in similarly ungallant fashion.

It was not until many weeks later that a few survivors began to dribble into Frizell's POW camp, PG 57 near Udine in Northern Italy. From these men he was able to piece together the tragic story of what befell those on board the *Nino Bixio*.

There had been about 700 men crammed into the ship's Number One hold when the two torpedoes struck without warning. In the hold, one torpedo pierced the ship's thin skin and exploded, killing immediately more than half the men down there. The hold filled rapidly with water and many more were drowned before they could escape to the decks. Many were badly wounded and unable to move, although the survivors rescued those they could reach. As far as we knew, not one survivor had been picked up by the escort ships as the doomed vessel's other holds began to fill and the ship floundered helplessly.

Miraculously, she did not sink. At around 1800 hours one of the escort ships ventured back to the scene and took the crippled vessel in tow. After several days they reached Navarino in southern Greece and after discharging the survivors she foundered in the harbour.

Records are not clear as to the total casualties in the *Nino Bixio*. One account says that of the 2000 or more aboard, only 300 survived. What is accurately known is that 118 New Zealanders died and, of the 200 or so Australians in Number One hold (most of them survivors of the Ruin Ridge battle), 37 were killed or drowned. The rest of the ship's complement were Indians, English and South Africans. Some nineteen men did escape in a rubber boat, but the sole survivor of that group was picked up many days later by the Italians. As Frizell concludes, 'As the story unfolded to the rest of us at Campo 57, those like the writer, who had drawn the right-coloured boarding pass that August day at Benghazi, realised just how lucky we were!'

The sequel to the 'incident' off Crete is interesting. *Nino Bixio* did not finish her days in Navarino Harbour. The Germans later raised the ship and towed her to Venice where she was sunk again, to block the harbour entrance. In 1952 the Garibaldi Shipping Company salvaged the ship and put her back into service as a cargo ship. The story does not finish there, for in 1980 the *Nino Bixio* visited New Zealand, calling at Timaru (the only Italian ship in living memory to do so) and Wellington, where a special memorial service was held on board. Survivors of the tragedy and relatives of the victims gathered on board for the service. A wreath was laid on the hatch cover of Number One hold by the serving Captain, Enrico Sambolini, who had himself been bombed by the RAF and sunk in the Mediterranean on Christmas Day 1942. It was agreed that the wreath be taken to Navarino on the ship's return voyage and placed on the memorial in the cemetery where the New Zealanders and Australians who lost their lives lie at rest.

8

Escape from Gruppignano

CAMPO PG 57 at Gruppignano in north-east Italy was represented to the prisoners by their captors as 'the best camp in Italy'. Their added arrogance in declaring the camp 'escape proof' provided the necessary spur to the Australian and New Zealand occupants, who rose to the challenge.

The camp, surrounded by alluring, snow-capped mountains, was situated on a flat river plain north of Udine in the province of Cividale. Just over ten kilometres to the north rose the foothills of the Julian Alps; to the distant west and north-west stood the mighty Dolomites and the Swiss, Austrian and Bavarian Alps. Yugoslavia lay to the east. By September 1942 there were some 2500 prisoners of war at Gruppignano, including 1200 Australians and 1000 New Zealanders.

At this time the camp was divided into two occupied compounds, containing several newly constructed sleeping huts, well lit, and with surprisingly good ventilation, which became a distinct disadvantage in the colder months, when icy winds swept down from the Alps, or funnelled up from the Adriatic. The huts were buttressed, ends and sides, with concrete footings extending outwards and with huge timbers up the walls and down to the ends of the footings. These triangles were spaced about five metres apart along the sides. The wind tore through every little gap in the planked walls and floors. There was a cookhouse in each compound, a canteen of sorts, adequate toilet and ablutions facilities, and an area for washing clothes. Water was relatively plentiful. Each compound was under the control of a senior prisoner NCO with a small but efficient administrative staff.

The official history of New Zealand in the Second World War, in the volume *'Prisoners of War'* by W. Wynne Mason (War History Branch, Department of N.Z. Internal Affairs, 1954), says of conditions in PG 57 at that time: 'There were plenty of Red Cross food parcels on hand . . . the canteen was well stocked and parcels of tobacco were beginning to arrive freely from New Zealand House and private sources.' But former prisoners at Campo 57 dismiss this as rubbish. Bill Kelly, of the 2/8th Field Ambulance recalls that there was only one time when they were able to buy food at the canteen: 'and that was one week when there was a local surplus of onions. The canteen catered mainly for tooth paste and razor blades.' The canteen was in fact a tiny pantry in the back-to-back kitchens of the two compounds. About two metres wide by three long, a small box-office wooden window opened to the outside. In line with the camp commandant's attitude to his prisoners, it was the smallest possible concession to the Geneva Conventions. Apart from the limited supplies of onions, there were occasionally some sweet toffee lollies available. The other items, which could be purchased using camp money, were mainly stationery, shaving gear and toiletries. Sometimes a thick syrupy wine and Nationale brand cigarettes were available, but these would be gone within minutes. Money chits, printed especially for the camp, were paid to the men weekly for use in the canteen.

Snowy Drew from the 2/15th Battalion was captured at Derna, and he spent several months in PG 57. When he arrived at Campo 57 it consisted of two compounds, each containing approximately 26 huts. These huts were of wooden construction lined with a malthoid type of material. Heating in winter was by means of a centrally situated stove fuelled by wood and coke. Each hut housed about 80 men. Bunks were of wooden construction of two tiers, four on the bottom and four on top. At one end of each hut were two separate rooms which housed the Senior NCO and Warrant Officer, the senior of whom was hut commander.

The Senior Officer of the camp was Major Binns, a medical officer with the 2/8th Field Ambulance—a South Australian unit. The Senior Warrant Officer was Arthur Cottman of the 2/15th Battalion. Arthur Cottman featured in an incident when the camp was first occupied. Camp Commandant, Colonel Calcaterra, ordered that all prisoners be given haircuts, but the men, including Cottman, stubbornly refused. Cottman and other 'ringleaders' of the revolt were handcuffed and tied to posts overnight. Facing further rebellion the following day, the Colonel ordered all available guards to fix bayonets, a machine-gun was set up, and small hand-carts bearing loads of handcuffs were wheeled into the compound. Those who still refused to be shorn were immediately handcuffed and placed in the detention cells, while the rest made a mockery of the proceedings, bleating like sheep to the mounting rage of Calcaterra. Eventually all of the men were given the rough haircuts, but they had certainly succeeded in enraging the pompous commandant.

Food, as at transit camps, was insufficient and almost inedible, but as Snowy Drew recalls the Red Cross were once again to the fore.

Red Cross parcels which came at irregular intervals were a great supplement to our meagre diet, which consisted mainly of a watery mess containing some sort of greens, with occasionally the addition of a little macaroni or sometimes mangelwurzels—a type of white beetroot. Everyday life was quite boring if one couldn't find some activity to occupy the time. Card games were a good pastime, the main games being bridge, euchre and crib. Once a fortnight, a hut at a time, we were taken to a bath house to have a hot shower. The only other highlights in the camp were the arrival of Red Cross parcels or the occasional arrival of new prisoners with fresh news of the war.

46

'Our first guards were Alpine troops, some of Italy's best', recalls Mason Clark of the 2/43rd Battalion, who was captured after an attack on German positions in the salient of Tobruk.

Our commandant was one Colonel Calcaterra, a sadistic fat little monster. This lovable character had a motto [emplaced over the gate], 'Cursed be the British but more cursed be the Italian who treats them well'. He made life as miserable as possible for us, and his chief delight was 'the boob' or 'Bastille'. This gaol within a gaol was built at one end of the camp, and the Colonel saw to it that no cell remained empty for long.

Commandant Calcaterra, a strident, strict disciplinarian from the Carabinieri Reali, ran Campo 57 effectively but with a heavy hand. Brutality was not discouraged among the guards, and the camp had a bad record over the ill-treatment of the internees. A.V.W. ('Bluey') Rymer, a wireless operator/air gunner from No. 70 Squadron was a little more succinct in his appraisal of Calcaterra: 'He was a short-arsed, fat-gutted little shit. If you were sitting on one side of the camp and you did not get up and stand to attention it was into the boob, bread and water!'

Prisoners caught in escape attempts were killed or wounded. Calcaterra prided himself on the fact that no one had been able to breach the formidable three-metre high, double barbed-wire perimeter fencing. Early in the winter of 1942 a New Zealand infantryman, Private Wright, was shot at close range while attempting to crawl through the wire at night. The bullet entered the base of the neck and there was no exit wound, which led to the suspicion that he was shot with a dumdum bullet. When this suspicion was conveyed to Calcaterra he paraded all senior NCOs in the camp church where he pointed out that in the First World War no prisoner escaped from Italy, and that none would escape in this one. Former Flight Sergeant T.E. Canning (3 and 6 Squadrons, RAF) attended the highly emotional meeting.

In regard to the bullet which killed Private Wright, and demonstrating a similar cartridge, he pointed out that it was a shrapnel

47

bullet consisting of a tube of brass encasing nine cylindrical steel pellets. When fired the rifling of the barrel cut the brass into longitudinal strips, and these, plus the nine pellets, went on their roving way. He claimed the projectile to be sanctified by international law, but it seemed to his audience that it was a considerable improvement to the dum-dum, at least at close range. He spent some time proclaiming that no one would escape from his camp, and the fate of Private Wright awaited whoever attempted it. The confidence of the Colonel stimulated ambition to prove him wrong.

Any schemes for crawling through the wire perimeter, which was well lit and heavily guarded, were regarded as both difficult and dangerous, so a small group of Australians conceived an idea for a tunnel. According to Eric Canning, the planning group comprised himself, Ted Comins (38 Squadron RAF), Dick Head (2/10th Bn) and Bill Kelly (2/8th Field Ambulance).

> In digging a sewerage pit in No. 2 compound the deep soil was found to be heavily compacted alluvium—far too hard for tunnelling—and it wasn't until a new compound was opened up to house prisoners taken in the battle of El Alamein that we were able to sample the earth under the hut closest to the wire, when it was found that the alluvium at a depth of about twelve feet was friable enough to enable a tunnel to be commenced.

Lance Sergeant Noel Ross (2/13th Field Company), a bridge contractor from Queensland, was in charge of the actual tunnelling. The tunnel, driven out from a vertical shaft, was to be about 80 metres long, starting under the floorboards beneath a central bunk in an empty hut in No. 3 compound. The hut was situated within 30 metres of the barbed wire, on the north-east corner of the compound. This corner was well away from any barracks or administrative buildings outside of the wire, so escaping prisoners had a reasonable chance of getting away undetected. On the other side of the wire, an Italian farmer had grown a patch of maize, and it was planned to slope the tunnel up gradually to the surface, with the exit hole in this patch.

The steady influx of new prisoners to the compound upset

the normal search routine, and the work went ahead unhindered. The tunnel team had earlier managed to steal a short-handled pick, and tin hats were used as shovels. The spoil was placed in boxes which were hauled back to the exit shaft, lifted out, and spread over the two-foot gap under the floorboards of the hut, or surreptitiously over dirt pathways and a cricket pitch being prepared for the new compound. The tunnel itself was about 30 inches high by 20 inches wide.

Mason Clark and two fellow prisoners were amazed when Eric Canning and Dick Head told them of the tunnel, and that it had been under way for several weeks.

> We were told that only the men actually working on the tunnel knew of its existence. Secrecy was a must, as there were some eighty Cypriots in the camp, and some of them could not be trusted. Once they knew of it, our Italian captors would soon be told. We had been picked as likely escapees, and because we were known to keep ourselves fit, with as much exercise and boxing as the meagre rations allowed, we would be handy as workers in the tunnel. Fit men were needed for the work; it was very arduous and dangerous. We three new recruits were quite excited that evening meeting our fellow escapees. The tunnellers were all Aussies and New Zealanders with the exceptions of two British-born 'Aussies', Arch Noble (2/24th Bn) and Scotty King from the 2/1st Pioneers.
>
> We learned that our fellow escapees had all formed groups of two or three, and several were going alone. All had made careful plans and had been saving some chocolate from the occasional Red Cross food parcels. Bill Thurling, Johnny O'Hearne and I had to start from scratch, but we eventually agreed on a plan to strike out for Yugoslavia once clear of the camp. Several of the others intended to do the same, hoping to meet up with the very active Yugoslav partisans. Some of the others intended making the long hike across Northern Italy to Switzerland. As we were situated north of Trieste, and close to the Yugoslav border, we thought the partisans our best bet.

Supplying fresh air to the tunnellers was a continuing problem, especially as the tunnel grew longer and the diggers moved further from the shaft. As described by Mason Clarke, the initial solution proved to be moderately successful.

We stole tubing and conduit from some of the toilets and wash-rooms, and made a pipeline from the surface deep into the tunnel. Bellows were made by some handyman, and so a new air supply was born. A man on the surface worked the bellows which pumped air through the pipe to the air-starved men in the black tunnel. Then too, flex and wire was stolen, the electric light globes taken from the centre of the hut, and light was introduced into the lengthening tunnel. We couldn't use lights down there during the day, unfortunately, as the power was switched off.

Once the tunnel reached a length of about five metres, the system for supplying air to the work face became ineffectual, due both to the small diameter of the conduit, and the fact that the diggers continually separated the taped joints while moving backwards and forwards.

Then the men hit upon the idea of inflating volley ball bladders to supply fresh air, as recounted by Noel Ross: 'They were pumped up at the mouth of the tunnel and then we would hold it in front of our face against the wall and let the air out. Due to the routine of the camp we couldn't work too long each day. Half an hour was the maximum time we each spent digging.'

Several cave-ins occurred during the tunnelling, but nothing too serious. Progress was slow, especially when clay was encountered. The men at the face worked hard in the mud caused by gradually rising water, the long drag back to the shaft with the spoil becoming slower all the time. They either worked naked or in some quite putrid old clothes kept down the hole; it was their choice, but they had to exit wearing their ordinary camp clothes. Fighting claustrophobia, muscle cramp and exhaustion, the men toiled away in the darkness, struggling to inflate their lungs in the fetid air, which caused them blinding headaches. Bathed in perspiration, their lacerated knees deep in the dirt and slop, their backs bloodied from continually scraping the roof of the tunnel, they drove on with grim determination. Each afternoon at a certain time tools were collected, boxes, bellows and buckets placed in the tunnel, boards lowered, and all dirt on the floor carefully swept away before replacing the heavy bunk. The retching, half-blinded diggers dragged clothes over their naked dirt-covered bodies. Singly and in pairs the men then slipped out of the hut and returned to their own compound. After a quick cold-water clean-up in the wash troughs, it was time for the afternoon check parade. Then a new complication arose, as explained by Mason Clark:

> Prisoners from the bitter El Alamein fighting began to arrive, and one evening a batch of new men were allotted to our escape hut. They were men of the 2/28th Battalion—all West Australians who had fought out from El Alamein, being eventually cut off and surrounded by hordes of German infantry and tanks.
>
> Our Sergeants visited these men the following day, and they were told of the tunnel that reached out from under the floor boards of their hut. They were asked for their co-operation, which was eagerly given, and sworn to secrecy. These gallant men proved dinkum Aussies, helped us in the work in the tunnel and sentry duty, and dirt disposal. With the added help the work speeded up and the tunnel was finished on time.

In fact the men of the 2/28th, gaunt and in poor physical condition from earlier ill-treatment, went to extraordinary lengths to ensure the success of the tunnel. They stopped all visitors at the door with the excuse that items had gone missing from the hut, and the person being called upon would be sent out to see them. The four men sleeping in the double-decker, side-by-side bunks over the hidden entrance to the shaft did so knowing that they would be liable to the harshest of penalties if the trap was discovered, but this did not deter them. 'Of course they were all for it', recalls Noel Ross with pride. 'They wanted to be in it, but the tunnel would only hold nineteen, and their health also ruled out their participation. They were in poor condition and looked like scarecrows.' In all, the tunnel took six weeks to dig.

Bill Kelly remembers one terrible fright towards the end:

> 'Pud' Poidevin, who would be first out of the tunnel, decided to make a visual check as to where it would break. While we watched

out of the hut window he poked a thick stick up through the ground from the end of the tunnel. But we couldn't see the stick, so the message to poke it higher was passed down the shaft. We still couldn't see it, so again a message was sent along the tunnel. Suddenly we saw this stick waving away about thirty feet across from where it was meant to be. We had a few anxious moments as the word was hurriedly sent down for him to pull the stick back down!

The escaping team, meantime, had undergone some changes. Mason Clark, weak with dysentery, was unable to escape, and his two friends would not go without him. Noel Ross, too, had to give up his plans of getting out; the Italians had found his reserve of escape food, and he was under observation. Bill Kelly, one of those who had first conceived the idea of the tunnel, reluctantly but gallantly gave up his place in the escape. Bill, an RAASC driver attached to the 2/8th Field Ambulance, had been given word that an exchange of non-military personnel was imminent, and he did not wish to jeopardise the chances of other men for repatriation. He had previously escaped from captivity twice, and felt this tunnel presented a marvellous chance for freedom, so it was with the greatest reluctance that he informed the escape team of his decision. 'One of the most courageous and wonderful men I have known', says Dick Head by way of tribute to his friend, who now lives on Kangaroo Island in South Australia. Two of the helpers from the 2/28th, Corporal John Costello and Private Stan Long, were given places in the escaping team.

In the early planning stages the escape leaders decided not to break the tunnel unless it was raining. They believed the guards would be less alert and seek shelter from the rain, and the searchlights would be less effective in delineating objects. But with the tunnel virtually ready to break the troops involved in the escape expressed their keen desire to go, irrespective of weather conditions. 'Their resolve was clear', according to Dick Head. 'Good or bad conditions, we can do it. There was an unspoken feeling—the greater the challenge the greater the incentive.'

On the afternoon of the break, Bill Kelly and Noel Ross placed a mushroom baffle made from wood and an Italian ground sheet beneath the thin ceiling layer of dirt and grass at the end of the tunnel, and using a bayonet cut an exit hole around the baffle while carefully planned diversions were taking place to distract the guards. This was then carefully lowered. 'I stuck my head and shoulders out for a look around', says Bill Kelly. 'It was a beautiful feeling; the air just seemd so much fresher that side of the wire. I felt very jealous of the blokes who were going out.' The mushroom baffle was then replaced.

That same day, South Australian Kevin O'Connell requested an urgent audience with Dick Head, Tom Comins and Eric Canning. He told the escape leaders of a twice-recurrent nightmare, in which he was trapped by a searchlight after leaving the exit hole. He was so genuinely concerned his dream might become a reality that he offered to withdraw rather than spoiling it for the remainder. The three men appreciated his concern, and in order to reassure O'Connell, who had been a hard worker in the scheme, they arranged for him to be one of the last out.

Mason Clark, whose illness precluded his own escape from the tunnel, described the successful breaking of the tunnel on 30 October:

> The escape was set for a moonlight night before the cold weather set in. The day before the escape we had a fright. An Italian appeared in the patch of maize and started to cut it. We watched him in anguish expecting him to disappear down our hole at any moment. To our relief he left the patch without stumbling on the hole.
>
> On the day of the escape, the last earth was removed and the tunnel was now ready. That evening Bill Thurling, Johnny O'Hearne and I went to the tunnel to make sure that no one 'jumped the gun' and tried to use the tunnel. The escapees came to the hut singly with their provisions. They looked a motley crew as they came in, some with old hats and berets, and an assortment of clothes. We lowered them one by one into the tunnel; they then crawled forward to the front of the tunnel.

All of the escapers had to be in the tunnel, closed with boards down, and the external helping team back in their huts by 'lights out' at 9.00 p.m. It was a time of nervous tension, but finally the nineteen escapers, plus the seven opening and closing helpers were all in the tunnel, stretched out uncomfortably in the cold water and mud. Although he was not supposed to know of the escape, a Catholic padre, Father Lynch, had made his way to the hut and blessed each man as he lowered himself through the floorboards. The occupants of the hut were singing lustily to drown out any noises, while outside the hut 'stooges' were posted to warn of any approaching sentries. Several men were watching the nearest sentry. If he happened to notice any prisoners emerging from the tunnel behind him and made to shoot, this team, under Bill Kelly, would throw stones at him to distract his aim. In the darkness of the hut nearest the machine-gun and searchlight other men were posted with stones, ready to distract the post if they opened fire. Mason Clark continued:

> When all was ready, word was passed along the tunnel and the first group crawled up and out into freedom. We all held our breath, but not a sound was heard. At intervals the others slipped out and away, to reform in their groups and slip away into the darkness. At last they were all away, and the tunnel closed and we were back in our huts for 'lights out'. The beds of escapees were made up. The guards and Carabinieri strolled through the huts and then lights went out. It was a success—after weeks of work, this was a thrilling moment. We laid [*sic*] sleepless, thinking of the boys making their way to freedom.

For one escaper, Kevin O'Connell, his recurring nightmares almost became a reality. As he exited the hole he was caught in the beam of a searchlight. Fortunately he recalled his infantry training: when trapped in a searchlight you 'freeze' to avoid a long moving shadow. He froze, his skin prickling, waiting for the first shots to ring out. Then the searchlight swept on, and he moved off undetected.

The dullness of everyday life at PG 57 was shattered the

following morning when word was passed around of the escape, and the wise took food with them on the early morning parade in anticipation of being there for some time. The Italians counted the men on parade, and finally they came to realise what most prisoners already knew—there were quite a few absentees. Parades in both compounds were subjected to a multiplicity of counts. The enraged Italians screamed abuse, but did not quite know what to do. Finally, they formed a squad of guards in a ring working around the barbed wire. They eventually found the tunnel outlet and a guard, with obvious trepidation, crawled back through it. Mason Clark:

> We were held on parade all day; our belongings were searched, and all other huts torn apart for signs of a tunnel. We had no food that day, and anyone who smiled was rushed to the 'Bastille'. However we cheered occasionally and booed whenever someone was marched to the 'Bastille'. The air was electric as prisoners became more rebellious, and guards fingered their rifles more itchily. One act of violence could have caused a general charge at the guards and the wire. We were eventually herded back to our huts.
>
> Activity was tremendous during the following days, as search parties of police and guards came to the camp, were briefed and sent away. Planes were overhead in the search for the escapees, and we were told that the whole countryside was alerted to watch for the dangerous '*Australianos*'.

From a distance the Julian Alps, thickly wooded to the snowline, appeared to present a reasonable refuge, but were in fact heavily populated. In addition to alerting local residents and the police, three divisions of Italian troops deployed in the region were notified of the mass break-out. The first two escapers were re-captured the following day, followed by others at various intervals. To make matters worse for the prisoners, it began to rain heavily. The lightning and thunder in the mountains was frightening, every clap of thunder had a thousand echoes. The rain was like an aerial river. 'It was like someone standing on a roof and throwing buckets of water over you', remembers Bob

Hooper, of the 2/7th Field Company Engineers. Two days after his escape, wet through and trembling violently, Hooper was discovered in the passageway of a farmer's home in Primulacco, eight kilometres from Udine. Some domestic fowls ('the place was a bloody menagerie!') set up a strident rumpus, and the owner confronted him with a trembling shotgun. The farmer, soon convinced that his sick captive presented no danger to him and his wife, led Hooper into the kitchen by the fire, where they drank Hooper's coffee and ate chestnuts while his clothes dried. The owner, with abject regrets, then handed the escaped prisoner over to the local police. This was to be the second of Bob Hooper's eventual seven escape attempts from captivity until he finally gained his freedom. His story is told a little later.

The odds were greatly stacked against all of the escapers, who were rounded up one by one; the last two were returned to Campo 57 on the fifth day after the mass break-out. The decision to escape in their uniforms, which made them all the more conspicuous, was certainly a big factor in the rapid recapture of the prisoners, but in formulating the escape plans the men had been worried that if they were captured in civilian clothing they might have been shot. The escape committee certainly did not want a massacre of recaptured prisoners to occur. As it turned out, the weather was the biggest factor against them, undoubtedly shortening their freedom. Heavy rain caused the already cold rivers to run quite swiftly, and guards were mounted on the bridges to prevent the men crossing.

Colonel Calcaterra was fortunate enough to have been away on leave when the breakout occurred, and he managed to apportion the blame amongst his staff when he was summoned back to take command of the camp. He imposed severe restrictions on the prisoners, and made their life more of a misery than before. Searches of the huts and the men's belongings became almost a daily affair, but he was certainly closing the gate after the horse had bolted. 'It probably didn't do his chances of promotion much good', declared Eric Canning. 'But he only had a short time to live, as word has it that he was shot by the partisans shortly after Italy capitulated late in 1943.'

Canning, Tom Comins and Dick Head, were fortunate in that they escaped the mandatory beating when recaptured by some Italian troops. The colonel in charge of the unit had himself been a successful prisoner escaper from the Germans in the First World War, and he sympathised with the three prisoners. He ushered them into a small village inn and gave them some food and drink until the Carabinieri arrived to take them back to the camp. The colonel was almost apologetic as he handed them over. Manacles were applied, and the men were loaded into a waiting truck. Unlike many of the others they had not been beaten on recapture, and returned to the camp unharmed.

The nineteen escapers, some of whom were first beaten severely in the camp cells, were stripped naked or semi-naked, chained, and given one month in the cells on reduced rations. Afterwards they were secured in a hut in an uninhabited compound, and put to hard, physical work. But at least they had gotten free of the camp for a time and, as Mason Clark reflects, were recaptured 'mercifully without loss of life'.

> We had achieved something, however. We had accepted the challenge of the 'escape-proof' camp. Our tunnel had done wonders for the morale of the camp; boredom was broken. We had shown defiance and spirit, even though we were wired in. Some of the information gained from those who had escaped helped the rest of us who were fortunate enough to escape later, so the long weeks of work in the tunnel and the escape had not, after all, been in vain.

Mason Clark was later permitted to transfer to a work camp, from which he eventually escaped and got clear away across northern Italy to Switzerland and freedom. Eric Canning summed up the difficulties inherent in any such mass escape attempt:

> The escape finished as most such episodes do, by recapture of the participants. It is almost impossible to plan movement in a hostile

country without assistance by at least some members of the community, and unlike the escape channels organised in France for shot-down airmen, no such possibility existed in Italy while it was an active member of the Axis. After Italy's capitulation, assistance given to POWs by Italian civilians under penalty of severe German reprisals was in many instances heroic. To the best of my knowledge our effort had the distinction of being the greatest mass break-out in Italy.

Life resumed at Gruppignano, but under far tighter security. Red Cross parcels were opened upon distribution and all cans were punctured by the Italians, both to prevent food hoarding and further escape attempts. As a consequence, all perishable food had to be eaten straightaway. While daily counts in most Italian camps were relatively lax affairs, in PG 57 the counts were a full military parade. Battledress had to be worn in the heat of summer, and in winter the icy wind sweeping down from the Dolomites and Julian Alps was bitter. Another wearisome exercise took place every two or three weeks, lasting a whole day: the complete contents of each hut were taken out, the double-decker beds dismantled, and all bedding and personal gear removed. The hut floors had been laid in sections and these were all pulled up in turn while the guards checked to see that no tunnels were being dug. Bluey Rymer comments:

Two things I remember most about Udine were the lice and the cold. The lice got into the lining of your clothes and laid their eggs. You had to pick them out and kill them between your fingernails. The bloody Sikhs in the compound next door used to pick them out and drop them onto the ground—they would not kill them for religious reasons!

Winter time was bad, especially at the 0600 parade. Blokes already ill from beri-beri used to pass out when it was really cold. It was so cold that the sentries on duty, in their half-closed sentry boxes on stilts, could not last more than two hours' duty; they stamped and screamed with the cold. It was the most goddam cold place I have ever been in my life. We were in a windy hut, and all we had was one worn-out blanket. It was even too cold to go to the toilet; some hardy souls managed to make it to the door to urinate, others did it in the aisles. Have you ever been so cold and desperate that you simply pissed yourself in bed?

Acts of barbarism still occurred at the camp. On 20 May 1943, Corporal Edward W. ('Socks') Symon (2/32nd Bn) from Kalgoorlie, Western Australia, was shot dead when he refused to accompany a Carabinieri guard to the detention cells. Symon, a capricious and knowledgeable lecturer at the camp, and a difficult man to beat in a debate, was a cool-headed stretcher-bearer who had distinguished himself by his unselfish heroism in Tobruk. During an attack on S.7 Post by soldiers from the 28th Battalion on August 3 and 4, 1941, a truce was called on the second morning to collect the dead and wounded. Socks wandered too close to the German lines, and was asked to tend some of their casualties, but having done this, the Germans took him prisoner. From the prison camp at Derna he gravitated to Italy, first to PG 66 (Capua) and then Campo 57.

On that fateful day, with Carabinieri guards patrolling amongst a noisy group of spectators watching a cricket match organised between two POW teams in No. 2 compound, Socks was cheering lustily as his 'E' team prepared the pitch for a long-awaited match against the 'A' team. 'You should have seen them rolling the wicket', Noel Ross recalls. 'Solemnly walking up and down, pulling a jam tin filled with sand!'

After saving his camp money for several weeks, Symon had purchased a small bottle of Italian wine at the canteen, and by the time the match started he was really enjoying the proceedings. Suddenly, one of the guards appeared in front of the spectators and began yelling and waving his rifle about. He was apparently motioning Symon to accompany him to the cells. The next few seconds shocked everyone, according to eyewitness Noel Ross.

We all stood up. Socks was a bit unsteady and the guard seemed to pick on him. A couple of chaps were steadying him when this Carabinieri stepped back a pace, brought his rifle to the shoulder and shot Socks through the chest. The bullet picked Socks up and threw him ten feet where he fell on his face, rolled over and said 'The bastard shot me!' How he said it I'll never know, but I was within ten feet of him.

'He shot Corporal Symon without any provocation', recorded an angry Francis Sullivan, a former private from the 2/15th Battalion, captured at Derna. 'Symon had made no attempt to assault him or molest him in any way. He had no need to shoot Symon in self defence. Two Australian medical orderlies and a camp doctor arrived and took him to the camp hospital. About twenty minutes later I heard that he was dead.'

Sergeant Arch Noble, meantime, had bravely confronted the Carabinieri guard responsible and told him in Italian to put his weapon down or there would be trouble. 'I didn't see the shooting, but everyone knew what had happened', added John Foxlee of Brisbane, formerly a corporal with the 2/15th. 'It was just cold-blooded murder. So far as I know, no one was ever punished for the death of Socks. I only knew the guard who shot him as "Strawberry Neck". None of us knew his real name.'

But the outrage of the shooting is not the only reason why so many former prisoners from Campo 57, including Noel Ross, remember the incident so clearly. 'The Commandant had promised a sum of 1400 lire and 14 days leave for anyone who shot a prisoner in the course of any provocation or escape attempt. Well, the Carabiniere got his leave, and Socks' official record shows "Death due to pneumonia".'

(In an earlier incident at Campo 106, Carpanetto, Private John E. Law from New South Wales was deliberately shot dead by a guard. Evidence points to the guard shooting Law after he had been bribed to 'look the other way' during an escape attempt over a courtyard wall one night. The guard was posted under the wall waiting for Law to appear just after midnight. He then shot the escaper through the head in cold blood. The Italian authorities there had a standing reward of 1000 lire and a week's leave for any guard who prevented a prisoner from escaping.

The guard in question was absent from the camp soon after for seven days. There is no indication that this man, whose name was given to War Crimes authorities after the war, was ever charged or punished by the Italians.)

Two of the Gruppignano escapers, Arch Noble and Bob Hooper, were part of a prisoner contingent later moved to Stalag XVIIIA, Wolfsberg, in Austria. From here the two men were transferred to a brick factory in Trieben.

Bob Hooper kept up his attempts to make his way to freedom; he was to make a total of seven courageous escape attempts before he was finally successful. In March 1945 he escaped from a hospital camp near Chemnitz and was picked up by an American Jeep driver who took him to an American unit at Chaleroy in Belgium.

The Gruppignano escapers

Australia

W/Off.	NOBLE, Archibald
Sgt.	WILLIAMS, Albert
Sgt.	POIDEVIN, Gordon C.
Sgt.	HEAD, Richard L.
Corp.	COSTELLO, John D.
Priv.	LANG, Stanley J.
L/Corp.	KING, David
Sapper	HOOPER, Robert St. Q.
Priv.	O'CONNELL, Kevin F.
L/Corp.	LIND, Charles
Priv.	DWYER, John A.
Priv.	COTTER, George
F/Sgt.	CANNING, T.E. (RAAF)
F/Sgt.	COMINS, Thomas B. (RAAF)

New Zealand

W/Off.	BOULT, Leslie F.
Sgt.	O'BRIEN, John F.
Spr.	NATUSCH, Roy S.
Priv.	BRIEN, Hector A.
Priv.	SLOAN, William

9

Breakout

F LYING Officer J.M. Kirkman from Kellerberrin, Western
Australia, was attached to No. 1435 Squadron, operating
Spitfires out of Malta, when he was shot down and bailed out
over the Strait of Messina on 15 February 1943. A Dornier flying
boat supervised his rescue and escorted the young fighter pilot
to Catania. From there he was sent in turn to Rome and a prison
camp in Sulmona, finally arriving at Campo PG 19, Bologna, in
north-east Italy. He was a prisoner of war for less than three
months when the capitulation of Italy was announced in September of 1943.

The news that Mussolini had been overthrown and his suc-
cessor Marshall Badoglio had signed a separate armistice with
the Allies gave Allied POWs in Italy a tremendous lift in spirits.
The subsequent capitulation offered many of them their first
real opportunity to escape, some having endured more than
three years behind barbed wire. Even the Italian guards were
elated as they acclaimed their country's armistice with the
Allies. They threw away their weapons, dressed themselves in
their old civilian clothing, and made ready to go to their homes.
Senior camp officers, meantime, repeated strict War Office
instructions that the restive prisoners were to stay put until
arrangements had been made to have them collected by Allied
forces. The Italians had declared their intention to defend their

charges against seizure by the Germans. But with a rapidly strengthening German presence in the vicinity of some camps, most camp leaders and senior officers were faced with the unenviable problem of whether to comply with very explicit orders to stay put, in what was fast developing into a confused and potentially calamitous situation. The outcome, sadly, was that tens of thousands of able-bodied soldiers fell submissively into German hands. The morning after the news of the capitulation had swept the camp on September 8, the wire at Bologna, instead of being unguarded, was lined by a German machine-gun unit which had moved in and encircled the camp.

The 'stay put' orders had unfortunately been promulgated months earlier, and were intended to forbid mass break-outs in view of possible reprisals prior to retrieval by liberating forces. But subsequent events meant that these orders were out of date and totally unrelated to the existing military situation. Jack Kirkman recalls:

> We were unfortunate at Bologna in that a German battalion was camped next to our POW camp. 'The Germans took us over immediately. A mass break was attempted in the hours of darkness on the same day. One of our men was shot dead and a couple or more wounded by German gunfire. I got so close to the Germans I could see their infantrymen lying prone with their weapons trained on us. We were unarmed and obliged to retreat.'

Before the German unit took over the camp and its administration, Kirkman decided to conceal himself before the inevitable rollcall and anticipated train journey into Germany. He confided his plan to his friend, AIF Lieutenant Jack Frost from Albany, Western Australia. Frost, by chance, had already discovered an excellent, albeit cramped 'hide', but his rangy frame precluded him from using it himself, and he pointed it out to Jack Kirkman. The 'hide' was a large rectangular cistern mounted high on the wall of one of the toilet blocks. While the Germans were rounding up his fellow prisoners, Kirkman was rapidly bailing the water from the metal cistern. Finally, he was done, and he hauled himself into the coffin-like cistern, bending his legs double before closing the lid.

By two o'clock the following morning he was suffering badly from cramps, having endured the confined area for over ten hours. But he had heard furtive whispers in English from the ceiling above him and, probing about in the darkness, he located a manhole. He tapped gently, and after a few moments the manhole was raised slightly. The four men in the ceiling took in Kirkwood's plight quickly, and hauled him up and through the aperture.

For the next 22 hours the five men lived an agony of suspense, listening to the sounds of activity and German voices below them; hardly daring to breathe. They had discussed the possibility of remaining there until the rumoured British landing in northern Italy had taken place and the camp was overrun, but decided instead to make a break for it. The choice was fortunate, as the first Allied troops did not reach Bologna for nearly eighteen months!

At midnight the five men carefully lowered themselves to the floor of the toilet block and scurried furtively across the dark exercise yard to a place where the wire had been cut earlier by other prisoners. Reaching this point, they flattened themselves against the ground and wriggled through the wire. Suddenly the perimeter lights blazed into light, and the escapers were frozen momentarily in the dazzling brightness. It was now too late for caution, so the five escapers ran for their lives, expecting to be cut down at any moment by a torrent of bullets. But no shots rang out as they sped off into the darkness beyond. Kirkman sprinted straight ahead for two hundred metres, then threw himself headlong into the welcome darkness and shelter of a bush, still expecting machine-guns to open up behind him. No shots came, but his choice of cover had been a poor one; the bush was a box thorn, and the prickles dug deeply into his arms, legs and body.

After a time Kirkman moved out and made his way to the prearranged meeting place, the farmhouse of the wealthy Medici family three kilometres from the camp. Here the five men were taken in and given food and coffee, then kitted out in civilian clothing.

Jack Kirkman eventually joined up with a tough partisan band which operated against the Germans and Fascists in the snow-covered Apennines. He remained with them in their mountain hide-out for three months before pressing further south to Arezzo, where he fell in with another group of partisans. After several adventures and a dramatic, bullet-torn crash through an Italian Fascist roadblock with several other escapers in a stolen truck, Kirkman teamed up with a South African major and they made their way south-east to the coast, finally reaching the town of Loreto. Here they joined a large group of escapers and, commandeering some ancient sailing boats, made the journey south down the Adriatic to Ortona, which was by now in Allied hands.

Kirkman spent his leave in Cairo before returning to Britain, where he completed a further tour of duty as a Spitfire pilot with No. 603 Squadron. When he eventually returned to Australia in December 1945 he had been twice mentioned in dispatches—once for his escape and partisan role, and the second time for his dive-bombing of German V2 sites. Jack Kirkman later moved to Melbourne and in 1952 graduated as a doctor.

10

Remembering Klagenfurt

A RBEITSKOMMANDO 10029GW was located in the suburb of Waidmannsdorf, on the outskirts of Klagenfurt,
principal town of the Austrian province of Carinthia, not very
far from the borders of Italy and Yugoslavia.

Not long after the Allied invasion of Italy in 1943, the
Americans set up airfields in that country from which to launch
their bombing raids on targets in Austria and South Germany.
The main base was situated at Foggia. For reasons of geography, it happened that directly in the flight path to their
intended targets—or so it appeared to the inhabitants of the
town—lay the town of Klagenfurt. Many hundreds were to die
in the later bombing of Klagenfurt and, comparatively, it suffered every bit as much as better known cities such as Berlin
and Munich.

Since the winter of 1943–44 the 300 occupants of the camp
had witnessed huge formations of American bombers passing
overhead on their way to targets north from the field at Foggia
in Italy. They felt reasonably comfortable with this demonstra-
tion of Allied airpower, although the planes frequently passed
directly above the town.

Lance Corporal Bernie ('Ben') Ryan was a member of the
2/1st Infantry Battalion when taken prisoner and was at this
time at Klagenfurt. He commented, 'In retrospect, I think we

realised that one day Klagenfurt would be attacked, hence some uneasiness whenever they came close. If we had only known what was ahead for Klagenfurt and, by implication, for us!'

On 16 January 1944, the airport of Klagenfurt was effectively destroyed by Flying Fortresses, but this was several kilometres from the camp and was, in any case, an obvious military target. A fortnight later, on 3 March, a group of seven Fortresses dropped 80 of their 500lb bombs in a field about 150 metres from the nearest barracks. The prisoners couldn't quite explain that one! Quite obviously, their camp was the intended target on that occasion but it was still not possible to come to terms with the certainty that they would have been annihilated if the Americans had got it right . . .

Meanwhile the town itself had not escaped the attention of whoever made these decisions. Up to 19 February 1945 it had been bombed some 50 times and although damage and casualties were considerable these were not major attacks. In fact, the men managed to convince themselves that this was about the level of aerial assault they could expect—nerve-wracking, but able to be survived, with luck.

February 19 was bitterly cold at around −20 degrees C, although not nearly as bad as the winter of 1941–42 when the temperature hovered around −30 C for days. But it was cold enough, and the usual morning mist had not lifted by 10.30 a.m., when the air raid siren warbled to signal immediate danger. German standing orders were for all prisoners to be marched from the camp to the nearest air-raid shelter. This was a tunnel dug into the rock and accessible by a downward sloping passage where a person could expect to endure as many hours of freezing misery as would elapse before the all-clear was sounded. The place was unventilated, often unlit, and packed with civilians, guards and prisoners. Having experienced these conditions, a number—perhaps one third of the camp's complement—elected to remain in the camp and take their chances. The German position on this was to turn an unofficial blind eye, mainly because many of them felt the same way. On a later count, Ben Ryan estimated that about 90 men remained in camp at 1040hrs when the gates were locked and the remainder marched to the shelter.

The first bomber formations appeared a little after 1100hrs, just to the east of town, winging their way northward, but slowly, more leisurely than usual it seemed. Then one group flew directly over the town and began dropping its bombs. 'Remember that this was only two or three kilometres from the camp, but in our fool's paradise we were not yet over-alarmed', said Ryan.

Then the real bombing of Klagenfurt began. From north, south, east and west, waves of the '*flieger Festungs*' as they were known to the locals flew in to give the town its introduction to terror bombing. Earlier attacks were minor episodes compared to the ruthless, systematic destruction of a city and the pall of smoke and dust rising hundreds of feet into the air must have made accurate bombing of targets out of the question. The attack continued through the rest of the morning and into early afternoon, and during all this time those who remained in 10029GW watched the not-so-distant carnage almost in silence. Some had taken to slit trenches dug inside the compound, most stood in the open, but all of them were beginning to realise the danger they were in. No one had ever thought of putting up a Red Cross sign (it is unlikely the Germans would have authorised it) and they now realised that the barbed wire, which should have alerted the bombers to the fact that the working camp accomodated POWs, would not be visible from the air.

About two o'clock that afternoon, what the men had so often told themselves could not happen, did happen. Only a small number of aircraft were involved, Ryan believes less than a dozen, and they approached from the north-west, passing over the long-since bombed-out aerodrome and the now-devastated centre of the town until they reached Waidmannsdorf. They were directly above the camp; they steadied for a matter of seconds, and then released their bombs.

For a short time there was no sound, except for the roar of the aircraft, but what appeared to be small clusters of silver foil appeared beneath the bombers. At first the prisoners took heart from the thought that this was the well-known trick of confusing the aim of the German flak batteries—which had been blasting away for hours with little result—but then they heard the unmistakable sound of falling bombs, familiar to them from the experience of being caught in mid-town during earlier raids. (It is a sound Ben Ryan describes as 'hundreds of trains crossing a culvert at the same time, and reaching its climax just before impact'.)

> I think most of us experienced that moment of blind panic when you realise life is about to end, but it passed and some, even as we hit the ground, took one last look and saw the actual bombs, scores of them, a few hundred feet above, swinging about in a crazy pattern like stubby silver pencils. In five seconds the nightmare was over, and strangely the moment of impact was almost an anti-climax.

It wasn't for some time that Ryan realised he had been thrown against the wall of one of the few buildings still standing and was apparently still partly stunned. It may have been this, plus shock, which made him go into the hut and put overalls on over his uniform—the working overalls marked K.G. (for *Kriegsgefangener*). Later, seeing the desolation of wrecked and burning buildings and knowing that dead and dying were still somewhere in the ruins, he and the others felt what they described as a selfish feeling of relief that they'd been lucky enough to survive.

The raid on Klagenfurt continued but no more bombs fell on Waidmannsdorf as the prisoners worked to free the wounded, some of them in the now-burning buildings, others pinned in slit trenches which had been crushed together so that the frozen earth held them until they could be freed with picks and crowbars. It was nightfall before all were accounted for—the dead, the wounded, and the survivors.

One tragic story from that bombing raid still haunts Ben Ryan. There were two 'nobodies'—foreign workers conscripted by the

Nazis to work in wartime Germany. The prisoners never learned their names, but the man was Dutch, red haired and slightly built, while she was a Ukrainian, of the same height but broad shouldered and heavier. How they met—perhaps working together—was also not known, but this unlikely, almost incongruous couple were a familiar sight running down the road, hand in hand, to the air raid shelter. On this day, knowing they would never make it to the tunnel, they took refuge in one of several large concrete pipes dug into the ground which were intended for use in just such an emergency. They were large enough to enable a person of average height to stand erect, but in the opinion of the prisoners they were little better than death traps. The pipe in question was just outside the camp, and one end received a direct hit, sealing it off at the entrance. A few days later, when it was finally cleared, the prisoners found their bodies, unmarked. They had frozen to death, with their arms wrapped tightly around each other.

In addition to the native population of 58 000, Klagenfurt was host to foreign workers and to some hundreds of Australian, New Zealand and British POWs. Four-engined bombers made no distinction between these people when they made their attacks, and the non-Austrian population of Klagenfurt was as much at risk as the locals. If it were possible, the 'kriegies' were even more eager to survive the aerial bombardments (by their own planes) than were those who might have been considered to have brought this devastation upon themselves. Be that as it may, every person in that much-bombed city was scared out of his or her wits and took flight whenever the 'warbler' alarm sounded.

To the south-east of Klagenfurt was a range of mountains separating Austria from Slovenia. These mountains were up to 3000 metres in height, and they presented a fine, if forbidding sight on clear, cloudless days. The distance from Klagenfurt to the Karawankens was around twenty kilometres, and the mountains beckoned as the best possible place to be during a bombing raid. Closer to Klagenfurt was a lower range of hills, which Ryan recalls were known as the Sadnitz, but it was for the more distant Karawankens that every fleeing civilian and 'kriegie' made when the feared warbler sounded.

The prisoners in 10029GW, whose camp was situated at Waidmannsdorf, a suburb a couple of kilometres from the centre of Klagenfurt, numbered about 300, and being an *arbeitskommando* (working camp) they were marched off every morning to their place of *'arbeit'*.

For most, the work place was somewhere in the town and, as the war moved towards its close and the bombing became more intense, the entire work force of the camp was employed in clearing a path through the rubble-choked streets. Not infrequently, this also meant digging into the rubble for bodies or perhaps to rescue the injured. This was done under armed military guard and at times their presence was welcome enough when bereaved and distraught civilians saw the ruins of their homes or the bodies of relatives. It was commonplace to be reviled and spat upon by enraged civilian survivors. Even in these circumstances there was sometimes an element of comedy, as when an elderly civilian, still wearing his swastika badge in his lapel, shaking his fist, warned Ryan's party that none would return home until all the destruction had been repaired. This was within weeks of the final collapse of the Reich, when even the most hardened Nazis had abandoned hope of victory. Ryan once again:

> I wish I could convey to you the extent of the total destruction of the centre of Klagenfurt—especially that section which bordered the railway and goods yard. Many a building stood as if sliced down the centre by a giant sword; three or four stories of flats, each one half a room with beds and tables and other furniture visible, the rest non existent. Or the sewers ripped open by bombs; or the railway lines sticking up at crazy angles, but miraculously repaired between air raids. This so that the railways were never completely out of action, albeit at the cost of the lives of many conscripted foreign workers.

Paradoxically, among the few structures left intact were the brick chimney stacks of factories. We watched them sway during bombing raids but never saw one fall. To be inside one of these, we thought, would probably be the safest place in Klagenfurt.

Perhaps it was not really so, but it always seemed to the prisoners that the bombers would wait until their working party had reached the most dangerous part of town before they made their appearance. Sometimes they would fly on to the north, sometimes a few would drop their load on Klagenfurt, swing around and return to base. Whatever the intentions, their appearance was enough. It was the signal for that wild scramble for the open country, foreign workers in the lead, 'kreigies' close behind—guards doing their best to keep up—then the civilian population, mostly aged, tailing the field. In winter the snow made the going hard and the hot Austrian summer brought its own problems, but away in the distance were those Karawanken mountains and the closer people got to them the better their chances of seeing another day. Ryan concludes: 'Well, that's how we of Arbeitskommando 10029GW ran towards those Karawankens almost daily—and survived. I often wonder how many of those young "gallopers" are alive today. Wherever they are they will, like me, always remember the running of the "Karawanken Handicap"!'

11

Witnesses to hell

F OR the majority of captured Australian servicemen held in German prison camps, life was relatively endurable. There can obviously be no comparing these camps to those of the Far East, where thousands upon thousands of men and women suffered gross inhumanities, starvation, and cruel death.

Until the final stages of the war, when Hitler's ungovernable rage saw many acts of barbarism perpetrated—and even condoned—on captured or escaping airmen, the Germans obeyed to varying degrees the strictures of the Geneva Convention. But there were other camps under German administration—the abhorred concentration camps, first set up by Adolf Hitler in 1933. While successive Australian postwar governments denied that our servicemen had ever been in these loathsome mass extermination camps, a handful of survivors are living testimony to the fact that not all our captured fighting men ended up in Germany's *Oflags* and *Stalags*, and were in fact sentenced to death for dutifully and bravely attempting to escape from enemy hands.

Very lights flickered in the sky to the west and south of Paris, and the distant sound of Allied artillery reached the agitated prisoners as they boarded the crowded cattle trucks on what was to be the last train to leave the French capital before the liberation.

The final evacuation of Fresnes prison, formerly the largest criminal penitentiary in the country, took place on 15 August 1944 in the face of the Allied advance from the beachheads of the Second Front. Five days later, British and American troops entered Paris.

A total of 1650 men, women and children were destined to travel on this train. Included in the number were 168 British and Allied downed airmen, who had been rounded up in the Paris and Beauvais areas through the traitorous work of a German double agent named Jacques Desoubrie, who had infiltrated the Paris escape network. Because all but a few of the airmen had been captured wearing civilian clothing they were not afforded the status of prisoners of war, and were sent instead to Fresnes prison, from where they were taken on irregular occasions to Gestapo Headquarters in the Avenue Foch. Here they were subjected to savage beatings, torture, and interrogation.

Nine Australians found themselves unwitting prey to the traitor Desoubrie and were tossed into Fresnes prison. Though the airmen made innumerable pleas for POW status, and their identities could have been easily substantiated, this was denied.

At the Pantin freight yards the prisoners had been escorted from their buses and transferred roughly into cattle trucks under the watchful eyes of their guards. The airmen still had no idea as to their destination, but one guard smugly informed them that they were being sent to a labour camp in Germany. The overcrowded waggons were of the '40 *hommes*/8 *chevaux*' type, but the guards crammed as many as 100 people into each of the 30 cattle trucks. On top of every fifth waggon was a wooden observation box from which the elite, green-uniformed guards could keep watch for escaping prisoners. Even before the cattle truck doors were slid shut and padlocked, conditions in the unlit, overcrowded waggons were hot and stifling. These conditions worsened once they were locked in, as the temperature began to rise and the air became stuffy and putrid. There was no room for all of them to sit down, and most only had a small handful of bread to sustain them. Little did the occupants realise that the cattle trucks were to be their home for the next five days, as the train cautiously made its way across France and into Germany. It was to become a nightmare of endurance.

Despite a valiant attempt by the French Resistance to halt the train before it left the country by destroying a rail bridge with explosive at Chalons-sur-Marne, the increasingly anxious guard company was able to transfer the civilian and aircrew prisoners to another train on the other side of the river for the remainder of the passage to Germany.

At an early stage of the journey several of the airmen tried to escape by prising up loose floorboards, but the Germans were alert to such possibilities and discovered the damage. Their officers threatened severe reprisals should anyone be stupid enough to try again.

Men and women alike, many suffering terribly from dysentery, had to endure the utter degradation of performing their toilet functions in a 20-litre pail in the middle of the crowded cattle trucks, and the stench, compounded by the lack of substantial ventilation, was appalling. As the toilet pail filled so it began to slop about in the dark interior, and the clothes of those unfortunate enough to be in the immediate precincts of the pail were saturated with the foul wastes.

The 168 airmen, dispersed into three of the 30 cattle trucks, were determined to escape despite the threats of the guards, even though many of the nervous civilians in their cattle trucks tried to the point of exposure to stop them, fearing the threatened reprisals. Eventually seven men slid through a hole in the floor of their truck while the long train was struggling up an incline, but the guards spotted them from their roof-mounted observation posts, and they were rounded up. A short time later a Prussian officer strode up to the offending waggon. He announced that, due to the escape attempt, a total of 35 RAF prisoners and twenty Frenchmen from one of the trucks would be shot. The chosen men were bundled off the train and made to strip naked. Two machine-guns were set up on tripods, and the first line of ten men ordered to step forward. Flight Sergeant Les Whellum (No. 102 Squadron, RAF) from Adelaide, South Australia, was one of those ten men.

> I thought, this is it, Les; goodbye to sweet life. I was staring straight into the business end of a machine gun, and my Lord, that hole looked huge. I can't remember whether I was frightened or just somehow resigned. It really comes as a dreadful shock when your enemy points a weapon at you, and you suddenly realise that your life might end right there and then!

But it was not to be; the lesson had been learnt, and to everyone's relief the officer ordered the shaken men back into the cattle truck. To make escape more difficult, all prisoners in that car had to strip naked.

Another time the guards spotted a young French boy with his hands on a tiny ventilation slot in his truck, trying to look out. One of them shot the boy in the hand, the train was halted, and the wounded, terrified youth dragged from the box car. He was then shot several times in the back.

On 20 August the train reached Weimar in Germany; the women and children were separated for transport to Ravensbrück camp, and the men continued on to a small rail siding at a place called Buchenwald. Buchenwald—Forest of Beeches— surely the most euphemistic of names for a death camp from which tens of thousands never returned.

The official International Red Cross 'Excerpts from Documents' records the arrival of the airmen in Buchenwald. A conspicuous annotation in the remarks column states *'Darf in kein anderes Lager'* ('Not be be transferred to another camp'), which meant that they were marked for extermination. Against their serial numbers is the further remark *'Terrorfliegers'*.

Beaten at random by sadistic guards and set upon by ferocious dogs, the men were hustled along a road known as the 'Avenue

of Blood' to the gates of the camp. After individual interrogation the men were stripped naked and had all the hair shaved
roughly from their bodies. The airmen were then issued thin
clothing bearing prison numbers and thrust into a special quar-
antine area near the crematorium, known as the 'Little Camp'.
Here they lived and slept on a small cobblestoned hill without
shelter. A few days later scores of young, innocent Gipsy boys
were removed from an adjacent hut and loaded on an articulated
bus bound for the gas chambers. The airmen took over their
filthy, lice-infested and overcrowded wooden bunks. They were
grateful for the shelter, but appalled at the manner in which the
space had become available to them.

Flight Sergeant Ray Perry (No. 466 Squadron, RAAF) from
Perth recalls that among other duties, one gruesome daily task
entailed going around the camp with a hand cart every morning to collect those who had died during the night.

> The bodies of the dead were collected on this hand cart and deliv-
> ered to the crematorium—not a pleasant task—but then there was
> nothing pleasant about the camp.
> The other prisoners were all very thin and we soon realised that
> the starvation diet we were on would quickly reduce us to a similar
> condition, so that it would only be a matter of time till we were
> wheeled away one morning on one of those hand carts. We weren't
> optimistic enough to expect the war to finish before our condition
> deteriorated enough to put us in that situation.

Pilot Officer Bob Mills (No. 78 Squadron) from Salisbury, South
Australia was another coerced into carting the dead across to
the crematorium. 'I actually witnessed these terribly emaciated
corpses being fed into ovens', he stated. 'It's a sight I can never,
ever forget!' Mills and three of his Australian crew members
(F/Sgt Jim Gwilliam, F/Sgt Keith Mills, and F/Sgt Eric Johnston)
had been captured together and all ended up in Buchenwald.
Ray Perry comments:

> We heard various stories about some activities in the camp but I
> didn't know if they were correct at the time, although I have since

found out they were accurate. The Germans had used many of the prisoners for medical experiments of various kinds. Some prisoners who had been well tattooed on their bodies were killed so that their skin could be removed to make into lamp shades. Life was very cheap in the concentration camps.

The sadistic wife of the former camp *Kommandant*, Frau Ilsa Koch (known as 'the Bitch of Buchenwald'), was the one who had these prisoners killed. The tattooed area was then carefully removed in the medical centre, treated, and made into lamp shades, decorative book covers, and other hideous trophies. Ilsa Koch's excesses and bestiality are well documented, but she remained defiantly unrepentant in prison after the war, finally hanging herself from the bars on her cell window in 1967.

Over the next two months the airmen fought a grim battle for survival, but they maintained a supportive unity under the strong leadership of their ranking officer from the New Zealand Air Force, Squadron Leader Philip Lamason, DFC. To a man, they behaved with proper military decorum. It was difficult however to fall into life at the camp easily; any small movement on the interminable rollcall parades meant an instant beating by a guard armed with a wooden baton, and the sight and smell of death pervaded every waking moment. Day by day they grew weaker, and began to fall prey to the many illnesses prevalent in the camp. Two of the young airmen eventually died through disease, hunger and neglect at the hands of the Germans.

Squadron Leader Lamason managed to contact a group of Special Operations Executive Officers held at Buchenwald, including the indomitable Wing Commander Yeo-Thomas, now known as 'The White Rabbit'. Lamason and Yeo-Thomas tried desperately to secure the release of the remaining airmen, but sad fate intervened when all but four of Yeo-Thomas's 37-man group of captured agents were taken one night to a cellar in the crematorium building and brutally hung by the neck with nooses made of piano wire.

Through his network of camp spies, some of whom worked in the administrative section, one of the survivors of

Yeo-Thomas's group, Christopher Burney, discovered that *Kommandant* Pister had also received orders for the extermination of the airmen. Burney immediately confided in Lamason, but said that he was almost powerless to do anything. It was obvious that the presence of the airmen in the camp was becoming an embarrassment to Berlin, and there was insufficient time and certainly no facilities or weapons available for mounting a mass escape operation prior to the appointed day. He did, however, manage to have a note smuggled out of the camp addressed to the officers at a nearby *Luftwaffe* airfield, telling them of the airmen illegally held in Buchenwald and asking them to contact the *Luftwaffe* hierarchy. It was an almost forlorn attempt, but the miracle came about. The *Luftwaffe* officers received the note, and it was sent directly to Hermann Goering, who was outraged. He intervened immediately, and by exerting extreme pressure managed to obtain the release of the remaining airmen.

Two days away from their date with the piano wire nooses, the airmen were suddenly taken out of Buchenwald and transferred to the air force POW camp in Poland, Stalag Luft III. Warrant Officer Tom Malcolm (No. 463 Squadron, RAAF) from Victoria was too ill to be moved, and was confined in the disgusting and unsanitary camp 'hospital'. He was delirious with erysipelas, a severe and highly contagious infection of the skin causing high fever and potentially grave complications such as pneumonia and inflammation of the kidneys. The disease was quite common in the hospital, and the potentially fatal malady could have been treated easily, and even eradicated, by the simple use of sulphonamides. But there were no medicines dispensed here, and Tom Malcolm had to endure the most primitive of treatments; he was wrapped naked in wet blankets. It was a kill or cure method often administered by the uncaring, indifferent attendants. Fortunately he survived and later joined the rest of the airmen in their POW camp, bunking in with Ray Perry and Jim Gwilliam. To this day Tom Malcolm has no memory of his latter days in Buchenwald, nor of his move to the air force camp. What he does remember, vividly, is being cocooned for what seemed an eternity in filthy, sopping wet blankets.

The Allied officers at Stalag Luft III were appalled at the sight of the crop-headed, gaunt and starving airmen who joined them after ten weeks in Buchenwald—men who flinched whenever a German came near, expecting a rain of blows.

Shortly after, with the rapid approach of the Russian forces, the Germans evacuated the air force camp, and the prisoners began a hellish three-week forced march through freezing cold and snowdrifts back into Germany. Eventually they were liberated as Russian and American forces swept through Germany and overran the temporary camps which housed them.

Today, most of the surviving Buchenwald airmen keep in touch through an Association run by Canadian Art Kinnis, who told the author of the men's feelings 46 years on.

The fact that no one knew where we were was always in our thoughts. We existed, and those who could block out their surroundings fared better than those who couldn't. To this day much that has happened has become hidden in our minds, and can only be recalled now with difficulty.

After we were released, and for many months, nightmares and sleepless nights were our constant lot. Some required more help than others, but we're all aware of the enormous help our wives gave us. Every man amongst us will be grateful to his wife till the day he dies for the moral and spiritual help they gave us when we returned home confused, angry, and filled with the terrors of that awful place.

Nervous breakdowns were not uncommon. It has only been over recent years that we have been able to resurrect some of the happenings to our sympathetic friends and those who were there. It was something of the past that we were afraid to disturb because of the consequences that might result.

Chest conditions, sinus and other problems that started then are still with us, and many still show the scars of the bed bugs. The mental scars do not show, but they're like that part of an iceberg which lays below the surface. Some have required medication and psychiatric help for extended periods.

Australian and New Zealand servicemen were also sent to a hellhole in Czechoslovakia called Theresienstadt, which was also known as the 'Small Fortress of Terezin'. These men were persistent escapers from regular POW camps.

Contrary to international law, they were stripped of their military uniforms and thrown into Theresienstadt. To all intents they no longer existed. Dressed in the now-familiar striped concentration camp clothing, they were put to work. During one working party revolt, the German guards opened fire on the prisoners, and slaughtered others by using shovels to split the men's skulls. It is virtually certain that several Australian and New Zealand servicemen died horribly in this fashion.

One Australian survivor, Wally Steilberg from Coffs Harbour, New South Wales, was held in a filthy cell in Theresienstadt, and has a particularly terrifying recollection of one morning in the Small Fortress.

> I got up around daybreak. The little courtyard was piled up with bodies, some of them without limbs or hands. It looked like someone had gone mad with an axe; there were human bits and pieces all over the place and these other blokes in the striped pyjamas were sewing them up in hessian bags. God, what a sight. What a mess!

On another occasion he received a bowl of watery 'soup', containing what looked like small cubes of meat. Steilberg recalls noticing one day that corpses were being taken in the direction of the cookhouse. 'To this day I think they might have fed us human flesh. The worst thing was you never knew when your number was going to come up. We made a pact that if they came for us we'd get one of them. I still have nightmares about it.'

Victorian Les Marsden tried to escape from the Germans nine times over three years. Sent to a concentration camp in Poland, Les remembers that during his internment 'literally hundreds of people died every night'.

Forced to endure hard labour for up to sixteen hours every day, he had to exist on a daily starvation diet of two ounces of bread and half a cup of watery soup. 'You didn't dare look at any of the guards in case they shot you', he reflected. 'You just didn't know your fate from one minute to the next. I never honestly thought I'd ever leave that place alive.' When he did, six weeks later, he weighed less than 40 kilos.

Another Victorian, Roy East, was captured on the island of Crete by German paratroopers in May 1941. Shipped over to Greece, he spent several months in the hellish, lice-ridden camp in Salonika before being loaded into railway cattle trucks with hundreds of other prisoners and taken to Stalag VIIA in Moosburg, 60 kilometres from Munich. Here, as NCOs, the prisoners were forced to join working parties engaged in such labour as building new prison compounds and using jack-hammers on a local tramway system.

In 1943, and due to an increase in bombing raids, the Germans bowed to Red Cross pressure by moving their prisoners to Stalag VIIIB at Lamsdorf, later relisted as Stalag 344. As before they were assigned to work parties on farms and in coal mines in Poland and Czechoslovakia. After an accident in which he was hit by a coal truck, necessitating a six-week stay in hospital, Roy East decided it was time to make good his exit from a working party. On 3 June 1944, in company with another NCO named Bert Driscoll, Roy East escaped. The two men managed to evade capture, but the weather was against them.

Incessant, driving rain deluged the countryside during their first few days of freedom. To compound their misery the men's plan to cross the Danube into Austria fell apart when they reached the river; it was nearly three kilometres wide and running fast. Crossing over in a little punt as planned was out of the question, so they decided to go through Hungary and Romania to Greece.

After three weeks spent sleeping in haystacks by day and

walking by night, the two escapers boarded a train into Yugo-slavia, but were picked up in a Gestapo search on 19 June. They knew the game was up the moment they were asked for some identification.

East and Driscoll were taken to a prison camp named Brno in Czechoslovakia, which was a political camp attached to Auschwitz. Here they were gaoled for the first twenty days and interrogated by the Gestapo every morning for at least an hour. Their interrogators wanted to know how the two men managed to obtain civilian clothing, German marks and bread coupons, and where they had slept and eaten. Another question they continually asked was how two escapers with no identification had managed to slip into different countries undetected. The Gestapo agents received the same unhelpful answers every day, and every day East and Driscoll were told they would probably be shot as spies, even though the men argued they had their army uniforms and identity discs in their packs. The Germans then tried another tack—they wanted to know if the two men had been dropped by parachute to do sabotage work behind the lines. Roy East recalls the questionning was actually not too bad as far as Gestapo interrogations go; they weren't beaten up, and in fact were given coffee, biscuits and cigarettes. After six weeks of this interrogation the Gestapo finally gave up.

East and Driscoll were locked in a small upstairs cell with eight Czech political prisoners. There were two single beds and two blankets between eight in a small, crowded room; the only ventilation was provided by a small window high up the wall. They slept on the floor, had no washing facilities, and were only allowed to go to the toilet in the morning. They were forced to use a bucket the rest of the day. Morning rations comprised a loaf of bread to be shared by all eight prisoners, and a thin watery soup at lunch had to last until the following morning. Roy East recalled the slow realisation of their predicament.

Almost weekly, army trucks took selected numbers of the civilians to Auschwitz and the gas chambers. It was always in the morning about 2.00 a.m.—never during the day. The political prisoners had a morse code system operating from room to room by means of taps on the wall, so they were well aware of what was going on. At first we didn't share this knowledge, but with our little bit of pidgin German we soon learned the awful truth. Until then we just didn't know about political prisoners being exterminated. When the trucks came for them there was a huge rumpus, with a lot of yelling and screaming, as they were well aware of where they were going, and their fate. I felt terribly sorry for them, but there was nothing at all we could do, and of course we were wondering when it would be our turn to visit the gas chambers!

There were no working-class types amongst the prisoners, and Roy East found them all to be professional people; in fact anybody who could have any notion of leadership, such as doctors, lawyers and businessmen. Nobody outside knew where these prisoners were; they'd just disappear off the face of the earth, and that's what worried East. 'Bert and I lived from day to day under terrible pressure. At any time we knew we could be taken out and shot. That was bad enough, but what worried me most was that my family would never know what became of me. We too would have vanished without a trace.'

The two men lived under constant fear of death for nearly three months before they were suddenly and inexplicably released by the Gestapo and handed back to the army. After a day in a prison cell in Prague they were taken to the air force camp Stalag Luft III in Sagan. There they were put in gaol and examined by the doctor; he ordered three Red Cross parcels each for them. East still remembers the immense relief in eating good nourishing food again after months of next to nothing. He'd lost nineteen kilos in Brno.

Later he and Driscoll were taken back to Lamsdorf where, amazingly, they tried to escape once again. The two friends were caught in the act and sentenced to fourteen days in the cells. However, as they'd already served over three months' imprisonment, they were released again that morning.

With the Soviet sweep into Poland, Lamsdorf was evacuated. The prisoners were forced to endure a five-month,

1930 kilometre march in freezing conditions west from Poland through Germany to the French border. During this terrible march the men received very little food, and none at all most days, and there was absolutely no medical attention. It wasn't just the prisoners who suffered, as their guards were also forced to endure the terrible conditions and lack of food. For five grim months the men plodded along, watching friends collapse and die by the roadside, unable to help them. Roy East has recorded his own problems during those awful months.

> I had terrible trouble with my feet, knees, hips and shoulders, which were full of rheumatism; bleeding piles, dysentry and snow blindness. The conditions were unexplainable; men starved and lived under atrocious conditions, marching the whole of winter through snow blizzards and sleet. There was supposed to be a sick waggon somewhere to pick up those who fell by the wayside, but I never saw it.

Kilometre after weary kilometre the men trudged on, hardly knowing what kept them going. After five months of frozen hell there was at least a faint glimmer of hope. They were finally reaching their destination on the Rhine river. But as the 600 frostbitten, starving survivors of this ordeal reached the town of Hagen they were informed that the Americans were crossing the Rhine and heading their way. The column was ordered to turn back once again.

This was the last straw for Roy East and another prisoner, George Bunting. Many of their companions, frozen beyond endurance, simply gave up and laid down to die by the roadside. The two men decided to play dead and fell down as the column straggled past. None of the guards or prisoners stopped; it was an all-too-familiar sight by now, and everyone was too weak to help anyone but themselves. Once the column passed the two men sat huddled and waited half-frozen until the Americans finally arrived in Hagen.

For Roy East the ordeal was at an end. But as with the Buchenwald airmen, he spent most of the next 40 years seeking rightful compensation for having been imprisoned in Auschwitz's Brno prison.

In 1963 Britain announced it had reached agreement over the claims of its servicemen who were held, contrary to international law, in Nazi concentration camps, and claimed compensation from the West German Government. Reparation was made to British servicemen in 1965, but when Australian servicemen made their application it met with stern rebuttal. The West German Government would not investigate their claims for compensation until a peace treaty to end the war, a war which finished in 1945, had been signed between East and West Germany.

Despite readily accessible German camp records, successive governments of Australia and New Zealand continually denied that their servicemen were ever held in concentration camps, and refused to even consider investigating claims by this handful of men. Their protracted pleas for some form of official recognition and just compensation were totally rejected or ignored for over twenty years. In the more extreme cases, this failure to act caused great distress and alienation among those who had already suffered so greatly.

It wasn't until 1987 that the Prime Minister of Australia, Bob Hawke, acting on the conclusive recommendations of a specially formed interdepartmental committee, finally gave the embittered servicemen an unqualified pledge of compensation for the time they had spent in recognised concentration camps such as Buchenwald, Theresienstadt (Terezin) and the *aussenkommando* of Auschwitz at Brno. The sum of $10 000 was paid to thirteen Australian ex-servicemen the following year.

The men's long and oft-times bitter struggle for due recognition of their claims, after years of governmental denial and inaction, was finally at an end.

The nightmares, however, will never cease.

12

A billion to one

ON the night of 4 November 1944, Joe Herman was on his 34th mission over Germany. Overall it had been a smooth operation, as the young RAAF flight lieutenant from 466 Squadron gratefully turned the Halifax B III bomber on a course for home base at Driffield in Yorkshire. His crew and bomb-aimer had performed well; their 11 000 lb cargo of bombs had aided in the destruction of a synthetic oil factory at Bochum, in Germany's Ruhr Valley. It had been a tense final run-in for the crew; twice before Joe Herman had been forced to peel off during run-ins after being coned by the probing searchlights and targeted by seemingly unshakeable flak. As he swung in for the third and final run to the target he did something he'd never felt a need to do before—he called his crew over the intercom and told them to put on their parachutes.

Curiously, despite his premonition, Joe was too busy to heed his own advice. He was wearing an observer-type harness, but his own parachute was held in a rack near the engineer. As they joined the bomber stream back to England, he began to relax. Suddenly there was a heavy thud in the fuselage and the bomber began to shake alarmingly. They had taken a direct hit just behind the rear spar of the right wing. Joe threw the aircraft to port in a desperate evasive manoeuvre, but his gunners quickly reported that no other planes were about, so he knew it was a flak strike. As he hauled the Halifax up again Joe saw the ominous reflection of flames on his windscreen, and his engineer reported that the aircraft was on fire. Then the Halifax was hit twice more on both wings. The six fuel tanks containing thousands of litres of high-octane fuel threatened to explode at any moment. 'Both wings were on fire. All I could see was a ball of flame, so I told my crew to bale out. The engineer tried to fight the fire, and my controls were burnt out.'

Joe scrambled rapidly out of his seat to assist and was just reaching for his parachute when he saw his mid-upper gunner from Tamworth, 'Irish' Vivash, crawling down the fuselage dragging a badly injured leg. A moment later his blood went cold when, out of the corner of his eye, he saw the entire starboard wing tear itself from the fuselage. The Halifax jolted, began to flip over, and then exploded, hurling the young pilot out into the night sky. Fate held nothing for him now but a four-kilometre fall to earth, and certain death.

He realised with horror that he didn't have his parachute canopy on. Death was inevitable. His mind was racing furiously, and he willed himself to seek the blessing of unconsciousness, but this was not to be. He was spinning slowly around amid tumbling debris, and he held a faint but absurd chance that he might find his canopy pack amid the dark tumbling shadows. But that was not to be, and he frantically scanned the dark ground, looking at the silver ribbon of a river below. Maybe, he reasoned, if he could land in the river . . . But it was a forlorn hope—he knew that impacting on water would smash the life from him just the same. He remembers praying as he fell. Suddenly there was a momentary collision, far above the earth's surface.

I hit something solid and immediately grabbed hold. I found myself hanging onto the left leg of my mid-upper gunner! We were floating down when his voice asked if there was anyone around. I told him I had his left leg and he replied to be careful, as he thought his right leg was broken! I asked him if he'd seen anyone else from the crew, and he said he thought the navigator and wireless operator were somewhere above. I remember saying 'Good show' and then fell into silence.

It seems that Vivash, also blown clear of the exploding aircraft, had only just opened his parachute when Joe arrived on the scene, after free-falling nearly three kilometres. The moment Vivash's canopy inflated he'd oscillated to one side, which was the precise moment Joe was passing. At the moment of impact Joe had clutched Vivash's leg instinctively, and had clung on with a ferocious desperation. Together they fell a further 1200 metres before Joe shouted a warning that they were about to hit the ground.

The ground impact was heavy. Joe Herman broke several ribs and suffered a fractured vertebra when Vivash landed heavily on top of him. Joe was the first to recover from the impact and tried to stand, but collapsed in agony. He took stock of his visible injuries; his left leg was badly injured and covered in bloody wounds, and he could feel deep cuts in his face and ears. His left flying boot was missing, and his left trouser leg was in bloody shards. His back and ribs ached intolerably and his arms were sore and bruised, but he still knew that they should move away from the scene as quickly as possible.

Joe tried to carry Irish, but dropped to the ground in pain. He noticed their parachute draped over a nearby tree so the two men tore it up and bound their wounds as best they could under the tree. Soon after they heard whistles, then the chilling sounds of gunshots and screams. It was the last he was to hear of the four crewmen who had baled out of the aircraft before it exploded. 'The three of us left in the aircraft when it disintegrated are the only ones who lived. The other four, who'd had time to bale out, were either shot or bayoneted that night. They were buried at Neveiges and later interred at Cleves, eleven kilometres north-west of Duisberg. They were unarmed, and were killed without a chance to at least fight back.'

They decided to move away from the area and headed towards a small hill with Joe, himself in great pain, supporting his gunner. From the top of the hill they heard the Germans examining the wreckage of their aircraft and the sounds of soldiers searching for other survivors. Beams from flashlights cut through the night. After some time the sounds diminished and died, and eventually all was silent. Carefully, Joe crawled over to the twisted wreckage, but could find no sign of his missing crew members. By chance, he came across his navigator's left boot and, as he had lost his own, he pulled it on. It was a little small, but he knew he would need it if they were to make any effort to evade capture.

> We laid up for a couple of hours as we were both losing blood. Later, we came to a big forest, where we spent the rest of the night. All we had was a standard-issue tin containing six malted milk tablets, six pieces of barley sugar, a square each of pressed peanut paste and concentrated black chocolate, and six ampoules containing 10ml of morphine to deaden the pain. We were on the loose in freezing weather, endeavouring to reach the Allied lines near Aarchen, for five days and nights despite our wounds.

On the fifth, bitterly cold night, the two men were sheltering in a barn when Joe discovered his feet had become frostbitten. They went to the farmhouse to seek help, but after washing their wounds and giving them some bread and coffee the farmer called the police, and they were thrown into separate cells in the town dungeon. Joe recalls:

> Later a Gestapo officer came in and I heard him beat up my mid-upper gunner. He then came to my cell, pulled out his Luger, and I looked straight down the muzzle. He hit me back and forth across the face with a cane stick he carried, and used every sort of threat, then slashed into my body as I lay on the louse-ridden bunk. He did this despite the fact that he could see I was badly injured, but I was past caring what happened to me.

On 11 November the two men were loaded aboard a sulky and taken to a small hospital, VI Reserve Lazarette, six kilometres from Dusseldorf, where their wounds were finally tended over the next twelve days. From there it was on to the Dulag Luft staging camp where Joe was questioned once again, albeit without the brutality inflicted by his former captor. His statement about the miraculous events of 4 November was transcribed and investigated. 'Even the officer interrogating me had to admit I was a very lucky man', he recalls. His terrible injuries were taken as evidence of the extreme trauma he had endured, and the Germans found no reason to doubt his incredible story of survival, especially with verification from Irish Vivash.

Joe Herman left Dulag Luft and spent four days at Bancau before being sent on to the Belaria compound in Stalag Luft III, from whence he later endured the terrible 80-kilometre forced march to Luckenwalde. He was liberated by Russian forces on 22 April 1945. 'An American Lieutenant came into camp on May 6th in a Jeep driven by a corporal. He told us that he had about a dozen trucks about four kilometres down the road in the forest. We were back across the Elbe that night and I was back with my English bride on her birthday, 13 May 1945.'

13

Kriegiedom potpourri

N EW South Welshman Jack Garland, from No. 97 Squadron
RAF, was a prisoner of war for three years, and like many
others suffered great hardships in German hands. Conversely,
there were moments of mirth and serendipity for the POW.

On one occasion he recalls that some of his fellow prisoners
had scarpered from the air force camp known as Stalag Luft IV,
Gross Tychow. And as any POW from Germany could tell you,
a successful head count by the guards in any camp was a rare
thing, and something akin to a miracle when they happened to
get it right.

The morning after a handful of prisoners had decided to take
their leave of the camp by jumping the wire fence, the guards
just couldn't come up with the correct tally. This was not only
due to the number who had fled, but to a lot of file fudging and
a concerted effort to ensure the Germans could not come up
with a true count. It was half serious, half game for the men.

The guards and their superiors finally began to show signs
of frustration, which became evident with a lot of shouting and
running around in circles. One can tell the temper of metal
when heated by the change of colour, and so it was with the
visage of the German guards. Their colour slowly changed from
a deep red to a livid hue; at that stage the prisoners knew that
their captors' anger was at the final stage before bursting.

Orders were shouted to the *Vorlager*, and trucks full of guards were disgorged into the compound. They scrambled around in some confusion before taking up their positions. The prisoners, who had been heckling these fresh reserves, were all herded to one end of the camp and asked to march forward in ranks of five men at a time, at five-metre intervals. The Germans now felt they were being quite cunning, and there was no way the count could be manipulated by the prisoners. But as the bard Robbie Burns once pointed out, things can 'go aggly now and then'. The prisoners, having been counted, strolled back up the *Lager*, slipped back into the column, and were counted a second time. Before the count was at an end, the number had already exceeded those held in the camp, and a long line of ostensibly innocent POWs still stretched out before the outraged officers.

A German soldier, according to Jack Garland, is hardly ever speechless, but they do go close at times—and this was one of those times. More orders were shouted, bayonets were fixed, and the guards formed two ranks about five metres apart, leaving a lengthy space between two barracks. A table was set up, and the prisoners were then 'invited' to approach the table where their identity cards and photographs were checked. They were then herded to a well-guarded corner of the *Lager* and kept under close scrutiny by armed guards.

'All this goes to show that counting sheep can be a very tricky business', stated Garland with a laugh, 'especially if you have a lot of obstinate sheep and rough old shepherds. A chore that should have taken no more than fifteen minutes consumed the whole day, and allowed our gambolling fence-jumpers that much extra time to be on their way.'

Another morning the guards were once again having considerable difficulty in getting the rollcall correct, and the POWs were once again having great sport in trying to make them look as ridiculous as possible. When someone escaped it was usual practice to pull the wool over the guards' eyes to enable the escapers to get as far from the camp area as possible. This particular morning however was different, as no one had shot through during the night, and whilst the men knew that the Germans were none too bright in the maths department, it was getting to the time when even they would come up with the right figure. One of them suddenly suggested a look in the barracks. Shouting and sounds of tumult issued from each of the huts in turn, and eventually the guards returned with one of them dragging a small, dark and thoroughly dishevelled fellow named Paul Anet, still wrapped in his blanket and quite unaware or caring about the uproar he had caused.

Paul had arrived in the camp at Gross Tychow one day from the Middle East. He had told the Germans that he was a Maori fighter pilot, but to the Australian and New Zealand contingent he looked as much a Maori as the Kaiser!

Paul was a small, dark lad, and told the men in the camp he could speak seven languages. Obviously from the Levant, Paul had strung the Germans a line to obtain better treatment than would normally be his lot. The Germans had placed him in Jack Garland's hut and, as he didn't seem to have eaten for quite some time, the occupants quickly organised a Red Cross parcel. Their surprise could only be imagined when he opened all the tins and packets, mixed the lot in one bowl, and proceeded to bolt the lot down his seemingly insatiable gullet! The mixed glop included coffee, meat, dried egg and milk, sugar and margarine. It was pointed out to him that Christmas was still a few months away, and the likelihood of obtaining another parcel till then was slightly remote, but this didn't seem to make any impression on him as he finished what was left in his bowl, opened his packet of cigarettes, and chain-smoked the lot.

The first night Paul Anet spent in the barracks the occupants had all gone to bed at the usual time and were peacefully asleep when, around one o'clock in the morning, they were wakened by an awful drumming noise coming from the passageway between the rooms. It sounded as if the entire Russian Army was parading through the camp. The door was flung open to reveal Paul Anet sitting on a plywood Red Cross crate, drumming his great number nines on the side of the crate. He was bundled back to his bed where it was carefully explained to him that being a 'Maori', and their room holding a preponderance of Australians, he was stirring up a lot of animosity with his 'neighbours' from across the Tasman.

The following night Anet's boots were stealthily hidden once he'd climbed into his bunk—but he was not deterred; he stole his neighbour's boots, donned them, and this time gave the barracks his impression of the Gross Tychow Tattoo. This time he became quite irate when confronted, and aired his knowledge of barrack-room English. 'I fuck all Australians!' he screamed. 'I take-a the knife, I kill all Australians and Englishmen tonight!' Being somewhat cautious and careful the men decided to take the man at his word, and had someone watch over him each night until he got it out of his system.

One day Paul Anet simply disappeared from the camp. It was rumoured around the grapevine that the Germans had finally put him in a straitjacket and had taken him off to a place with padded walls. 'I hope he survived the war', says Garland, 'but knowing the German penchant for disposing of troublesome people with addled brains I don't hold out much hope that the poor sod celebrated VE Day'.

In another of Garland's camps, this time Stalag Luft I in Barth, *Hauptman* Müller was the *Kommandant* in what the prisoners laughingly referred to as their 'holiday camp by the sea'. A very affable fellow, it was rumoured that Müller was married to an Englishwoman and had been educated at Eton. He certainly spoke better English than most of the camp inmates, and seemingly had not been indoctrinated with the streak of sadism that most of those associated with the National Socialist Party took as their divine right.

One morning at *Appell* (rollcall), *Hauptman* Müller walked into the compound with a cardboard box under his arm, and after the usual salutations he proclaimed 'I have something here that you have been requesting'. He placed the box on the ground, removed the lid, and out tumbled two half-grown kittens. The prisoners did actually have a problem with rodents in the camp, and the well-meaning Müller had seen this as the solution.

The kittens were seen around the *Lager* for a couple of weeks, no doubt being taught their duty in keeping the rodent population to a minimum. It was then noticed that they no longer put in an appearance at their favourite haunts. Thereafter, the most asked (but never answered) question in the camp became 'Who was the rotten mongrel who had the kitten pie?'

Normally at the cry of 'Goon in the block!' (indicating a guard entering the barracks), ways would be found to divert the intruder from his purpose, which usually entailed catching the prisoners at doing something forbidden. This particular day, as the guard walked uninvited into Garland's room, a game of table tennis was in progress. The audience were all sitting around on their beds, and their heads were going backwards and forwards with the passage of play. The opponents were playing shot for shot, and the excitement had everyone agog. 'The goon watched, and his head also went with the play. Finally he scratched his head and strode out through the door muttering to himself in disbelief. No wonder—there had been no bats, no ball, and no net!'

Private Alfred Passfield (2/11th Bn) made an incredible eight breaks from captivity in Germany, culminating in his successfully reaching the Allied lines in May 1945. Captured during the invasion of Crete in 1941, the West Australian infantryman was sent to Stalag VIIA, Moosburg. Over the next eighteen months Passfield got away from the camp on no less than four occasions; the first by slipping away from a working party, the second through a sewer drain, the third by cutting through the perimeter wire, and the fourth by exchanging identities with another prisoner. On each occasion he got clear of the camp and was on the loose for several days. At a small station between Oppeln and Lamsdorf he leapt from a train. He was picked up in a railway subway four days later. Sent to work near an aerodrome at Gleiwitz, Passfield donned civilian clothes and was once again on the loose. This time he made it as far as Komarom on the Hungarian–Czech border before being captured by an alert policeman.

Taken to Transit Lager 172 near Belgrade to await transportation to Germany, Passfield attempted to escape through the damaged barbed-wire fence following an air-raid, but was quickly recaptured. His next place of imprisonment was Rosengraben, in the Austrian Alps, where he wasted little time in slipping out through a window. But this last escape attempt was also doomed to failure; after his recapture he was sent off to a working camp attached to Stalag XVIIIA, Wolfsberg. Eventually this camp lay in the path of the Allied advance and the guards stationed there became increasingly less vigilant. As a consequence Alf Passfield and several other prisoners virtually walked out of the camp and caught a lift on a hospital train headed west. At Innsbruck they came across the American forces and made their identities known. After four years' captivity and eight spirited attempts to escape, Arthur Passfield was finally free.

Passfield was an 'escape artist' in more than one sense of the phrase. Boredom in the camps led to his taking up the art of tattooing, and as he became more adept his talent was much in demand. At each camp he asked someone to sketch local landmarks which he then copied onto his own body. When not tattooing his fellow prisoners, he could be found painstakingly inking designs onto himself, so that by war's end his body was covered in several dozen remarkable tattoos illustrating his life as a prisoner of war. He now laughingly refers to himself as 'a walking art gallery'.

At one stage of his life as a POW, and because of his record as an inveterate escaper, he found he could only apply for work in a *Strafelager* (punishment camp) instead of the general working parties to which NCOs were allocated. He was able to put his name down for railway work at Heiflau, near Wolfsberg in southern Austria, which was supposed to entail duties only marginally worse than an ordinary working party. With increased Allied bombing on the railways towards the end of the war, it wasn't long before the railway system had all but closed down, but this in turn meant food rations were not able to get through to the more remote areas as frequently as before. Passfield recalls:

We had a lot of spare time and, with the planes rumbling overhead and a man's guts rumbling inside for the want of victuals, one had to do something to pass the time, so once more I took to the tattooing. I put some on myself, and several on others. There was a church in the village . . . I got a bloke to sketch it and tattooed the design on myself. I had just about reached the limit for tattooing myself as I had no more room I could reach comfortably. In fact I had to do some contortions to put the last ones on. However, I was never short of customers, and this was especially noticeable when the grub was short. It was the same in all the camps. When men are hungry they cannot settle to read or do anything else, but the tattooer's needle took their minds off the emptiness of their bellies.

I made sure *my* [*emphasis added*] needles did, at least. I was as rough with my customers as I was with myself, for I always reckoned the blood must flow for a good clear design afterwards. Later, on the boat returning to Australia, I tattooed a lot of English sailors, and also three W.R.E.N.S., and got the nickname of the 'Beast of Belsen'. Coming through the tropics, what with the heat and the pain of the needle, a good many would pass out, and I would say 'Stick him under the table until he comes to. Next please!'

14

Reflections

R ALPH Coutts was born in Devon, England, and when taken prisoner was serving with the Kings Own Royal Norfolk Yeomanry, 65 Anti-Tank Regiment. He emigrated to Queensland after the war, and subsequently has been actively involved as an office-bearer in several RSL and Ex-POW associations. As a prisoner of the Italians and Germans, his impressions of both captors are worth recording.

The Italians were a gentle people, most of whom did not want war, and would have been quite satisfied if left to get on with their lives without interference. There was, of course, a small hard core of dedicated Fascists, most of whom I suspect were self-seeking and who had no particular feeling for the hopes and aspirations of the largely peasant remainder of the population. Many, or perhaps I should say most, of the men who managed to escape and spend some time moving around Italy, received food and assistance from the ordinary people, and few were ill-treated or handed over to the authorities.

Certainly in most cases the Italian Navy, Air Force and Army had not put up much of a show, and had been quite easily defeated. I can speak with no sort of authority on the Navy or Air Force, but I suspect that my remarks regarding the Army, with which I had come in contact, would apply generally to the other services.

My impression was that the average Italian did not want to be a soldier, or take part in a war, and most of those taken prisoner or surrendering in the Western Desert campaigns seemed to be delighted to be taken prisoner and out of the war. Some units fought bravely and tenaciously, as the Indian Divisions found out at Keren in Ethiopia, probably units of the regular army, but such conduct was not usual. On the whole they were badly equipped, badly trained and badly led, and there was a vast gulf between the men and their officers. It seemed that whatever the conditions, and how extended the lines of communication, the officers had nothing but the best while the men lived at an extremely low level.

The treatment we received from the Italians as prisoners of war was generally as fair and humanitarian as could be expected under the circumstances, and I cannot recall one instance of actions of spite or brutality towards a prisoner of war. At the time I thought that they were a miserable, cowardly lot; now I like the Italians as a happy and gentle people; all the waving of arms and shouting during an argument is seldom followed by violence, and they are men after my own heart—they don't like war.

The English have a bawdy, almost obscene sense of humour which is redeemed by its subtlety; the Scots have a dour, dry humour; the Welsh an oblique sort of humour; the Irish of course a twisted humour which is often used against themselves; American humour is of the straight-forward slapstick type; the stolid German appears to have little, if any sense of humour, which probably accounts for much of their history.

Admittedly by 1944 they had little to laugh about, and the only time I saw any of them doubled up with laughter was when I committed a *faux pas* in German grammar; at the time I considered it only mildy humorous, and certainly not side-splitting. One of the members of my team at Bm3 was belittling me to the Germans. I was soft and only a clerk, but I certainly wasn't going to put up with this. It was quite fortuitous that a short time before he had told me that he had been taken prisoner without having fired a shot at the enemy, and he was an infantryman from the First Army which had operated in Tunisia. I therefore had my ammunition given to me, and I proceeded to tell the Germans that he had nothing to shout about as he had never shot at the enemy. Unfortunately I used the wrong past participle—*geschissen* instead of *geschossen*, and what I told them in effect was that he had never shit at the enemy. They absolutely rolled around with mirth.

They were absolute martyrs to anyone in uniform, or any published order or prohibition, and would obey such persons or orders without hesitation or question as if they might be holy writ. It seemed they were unable to comprehend the British, who not only questioned men in uniform and orders or prohibitions, but actually ignored them; perhaps they admired in us the courage that was not in them.

They were unhappy when they had no job to do, and were industrious and conscientious workers who would stick out the job until it was finished, no matter how difficult, dangerous or obnoxious, and would no more have thought of slacking or trying to get out of any part of it than they would of running naked down the High Street.

Although at times they appeared to tell and enjoy dirty stories they had an almost Victorian prudery; in any case they were completely unable to appreciate any of our alleged funny tales. Most of the Germans had heard certain English words used with great frequency, and eventually it became fairly clear to them that these were our swear words, and started to query us as to the words and their meanings. German swearing is fairly innocuous, mainly in the terms of animals, and to call a German a criminal was like an Englishman (not an Australian) calling someone a bastard, which was about the limit. They learned what the big 'F' word meant, but could not understand its use as a swear word, particularly when it was used as a noun, a verb and an adjective.

The Russians and other Eastern Europeans they treated as animals. Other Europeans, Asiatics and Americans they treated as third-class citizens, except for the British. I have been unable to reconcile this attitude; nevertheless it was true that of all the internees and prisoners of war, only the British were treated with any sort of deference or equality, and it seemed that somehow they had tacitly acknowledged the superiority, or at least equality of the British. I am unaware if this same attitude was extended to other members of the Commonwealth, such as New Zealanders and Australians, but I can assure you that as far as we were concerned we were the best treated, least abused, and least heavily worked of prisoners.

I have still not come up with a general assessment of the character, and I am afraid I never will. I think that they are the only nation with which I have been associated of which I have not been able to reach a definite conclusion; maybe they are such an indefinite people.

Since the war I have never come across a German who was a member of the Nazi Party, unless they did not believe in it or Hitler but joined to protect their job or prospects; nor have I found one who will admit to knowing, during the war, of the existence of the concentration camps or what atrocities went on inside their fences.

102

It must have been a great shock and surprise when they failed to reach Moscow by Christmas 1941 or 42 and later at the disaster of Stalingrad, and the still later defeat of their army by the Russians, the **Untermenshen**, who drove them back into Germany. I have little sympathy for that generation of Germans.

Jim McCauley (2/15th Bn, 9th Division) spent four years and one month as a prisoner in Italy, Germany and Poland. He was captured in Libya on 7 April 1941 during the Benghazi Retreat, better known to the Australians as the 'Benghazi Handicap'. McCauley was finally released in Austria on 11 May 1945 by Patton's Fourteenth Army, after being on the run for two months. After returning to his home in Hughenden, North Queensland, he was discharged at the end of September 1945. He reflected:

After discharge from the Army the hardest thing was to settle down to civilian life. You felt you were unwanted. You had done nothing during the war and you just wanted to keep moving all the time. This was the attitude of the ex-POW; after his release from captivity, after so many lost years, there was so much that one had to do to make up.

We were not like the Diggers who had returned from the Middle East and New Guinea; we didn't want to be paraded through the streets to cheering crowds. We felt we had done nothing and wanted just to get out of the Army, come home unnoticed, meet our loved ones, and try to settle down. For us the war was over the day we were taken prisoner.

I shall never forget my experience as a POW, even if I live to be a hundred. One of the greatest experiences was mateship. You had a good mate, you helped one another, shared everything together, and this comradeship still exists today though a lot of our mates have since passed on. You will never forget your mate—one of the things that helped pull one through.

Jack Champ, formerly of the 2/6th AIF, was captured on the small island of Milos while escaping from the Germans in Greece. Involved in many daring escapes, Champ saw out the last months of his POW life in the castle prison, Oflag IVC, Colditz.

How was one affected in after life, having been a prisoner of war? Generally speaking, whilst it was most unpleasant to be deprived of one's liberty for four years, and to live with the constant uncertainty of the eventual conclusion, there were certain benefits which were an inherent result.

Firstly, being a prisoner of war made one appreciate the everyday things in life which would otherwise be taken for granted, and easily dismissed as normal. These include the freedom to walk unhindered along a street, to go to the cinema or theatre, to play golf, go sailing, or enjoy a swim. To sit down at a table and eat as much as you like of your favourite food, surrounded by your loved ones. To be able to post and receive a letter which has not been read and censored by a stranger, and so many thousands of other everyday activities which we all enjoy in our democratic environment. This, after all, is why we went to war—to be able to preserve and always enjoy the simple liberties one should expect in this vast and glorious world.

I am sure that all former prisoners of war acquired a completely new set of values. We learned to be tolerant. Forced to live in cramped quarters, close to one's fellow man with all his habits and idiosyncrasies for a long period of time is a real test of one's tolerance. Without this tolerance none of us would have lasted for very long at all, and this same tolerance flowed through into our later civilian lives. I do believe (although some wives may not agree!) that the majority of ex-prisoners of war proved to be relatively easy to live with.

Finally, without exception, we cemented lasting friendships of lifelong tenancy.

Part II
Australian POWs in Singapore, Thailand and Japan

15

The fall of Singapore

BY 13 February 1942, Singapore was in its death throes. Most of the two brigades of the Australian 8th Division had been squeezed into an oval, about seven miles in circumference, a few miles from the city. Japanese bombers in groups of from nine to 54 flew continuously overhead, unopposed, and the streets were congested with military traffic and about a million defenceless civilians.

That night, the guns of 60 Battery of the 2/10th Field Regiment were firing from a position in a small park at Japanese troops and guns on Bukit Timah which overlooked most of the island.

As battery surveyor I was resting with my team of four gunners behind the command post, listening to the roar of the 25-pounders and watching the muzzle flashes light up the whole area. To get to this position we had driven a few miles along clogged roads, stopping frequently to move dead civilians and wrecked rickshaws out of our path. Suddenly the Battery Captain emerged from the darkness. 'We're nearly out of ammo', he said. 'But I gather there's an ammunition dump at Alexandra not far away. Could you get over there and see what you can find.'

Gunner Tom Elstobb, my driver, was a tall former shearer from western Queensland and a very resourceful soldier. He stood up and stretched. 'Our survey truck's a bit small', he said. 'I'll poke around and look for something a bit bigger.'

Within half-an-hour he was back, driving an enormous furniture removal van. Gunners Little, Elliot and Smeaton and I climbed aboard and we set off for the island's largest ammunition magazine. When we finally found it there was no one there except a few frightened Tamils who could tell us nothing.

Lighting our way with a torch, we walked through numerous long tunnels containing all kinds of ammunition, ranging from six and nine-inch naval shells down. Finally we came upon a stack of rectangular steel cases, each containing four 25-pounder shells. With the reluctant help of the Tamils we loaded the van and drove slowly back to the gun position.

By this time a heavy Japanese gun had begun ranging on to 60 Battery, the guns of which were wheel to wheel. Japanese shells passed overhead making a rushing noise like a train before exploding with a terrific crump behind us. Our gunners referred to their opponent as 'Asiatic Annie'.

Before dawn we were on the move again, only to be caught up in a traffic jam near a crossroads. Soon a swarm of Japanese bombers appeared heading our way. From the protection of a deep stormwater drain we watched the planes lift as they released their cargo, and waited as the bombs screamed down on the rows of houses on each side of the street.

When the deafening detonations of the bombs ceased we emerged cautiously into a dense cloud of smoke and falling debris to find our survey truck a twisted wreck.

'Wait here', Tom Elstobb said. 'I'll poke around and see what I can find.' Not long afterwards he returned driving a big British Army Rolls Royce armoured car. 'They must have taken out the guns', he apologised. 'But there's a case of brandy in the back.'

Shells and bombs continued to rain on the city, which burned under a thick black canopy of smoke from flaming oil tanks and buildings. The numbers of dead increased. We were told by the Battery Captain that it could soon be a case of every man for himself. The water supply which came from Johore Bahru was in Japanese hands. We were almost out of artillery ammunition. We were down to rifles, bayonets and grenades.

On Sunday afternoon 15 February we were given the order 'prepare to advance'. 'About bloody time', I heard all around me as we headed for Tanglin Hill. As we proceeded, an eerie silence settled over the darkened city. The bombing and shelling ceased and the silence was loud—broken only by the occasional crackle of small-arms fire.

At Tanglin Hill we were told it was all over. In shocked disbelief some men cried with rage; some moved off in small groups hoping for some way of escape; most finally fell into a sleep of exhaustion, few having slept much since the Japanese landing on the island on 8 February 1942.

Next day a few curious Japanese soldiers appeared on the outskirts of our area while we were busy rendering our arms and equipment unfit for further use. Later we were told that we would be walking to Changi, some eighteen miles distant, on the following afternoon.

It was a humiliating march, through crowds of victorious Japanese soldiers and stunned civilians. My group was led by six Gordon Highlanders in full kilts, their bagpipes wailing a highland lament.

One other memory of that exhausting march which remains with me is of the bodies of two Ghurkas stuck upright in a hedge as though the moment of their death had been frozen in time.

I reached Changi in the early hours of the morning and collapsed with exhaustion on a football field. Changi, now the site of Singapore's international airport, was then a vast area of barracks and cottages which had housed the British garrison and dependants. When we entered it, it was a green and gracious place adorned with coconut trees, gardens and hedges.

With my scanty possessions I found myself with twelve other men of my old unit in a room large enough to house six.

My first job at Changi was to lead a burial party to bury eighteen Chinese civilians at a nearby kampong. They had been tied up and shot by Japanese troops clearing the Changi area of civilians.

Life soon settled into a routine. The main ingredients were hunger and boredom. One virtue of Changi was that the Japanese guards remained outside the camp, the administration being left to our own officers.

Units scattered during the fighting were reunited in Changi in their original formations.

Our doctors warned that the lack of vitamins in our diet would lead to severe problems, among them the onset of impotence. They suggested that various plants growing around the camp— such as hibiscus—could provide some of the vitamins needed. In no time there was not a leaf on the once magnificent hibiscus hedge surrounding our cottage.

For me, Changi was an interlude. After about six weeks there was a call for volunteers to join a working party to be moved to a new camp in Singapore. Being a believer in the saying that 'the devil you don't know might be better than the one you do', I volunteered to join.

16

The Great World

BEFORE World War II, one of the brightest amusement parlours in Singapore was The Great World. Bathed in a blaze of light, it was a world apart from life in adjoining Singapore once darkness fell.

Within its bounds were a large cabaret and numerous picture theatres which catered for Indian, Chinese, Malay and English-speaking patrons. There was a Chinese theatre, with its elaborate costumes, its noisy sound effects and its 'invisible' man in black, who shifted the props as the drama unravelled. There were peep shows, shooting galleries, beer gardens, shops and stalls of infinite variety, gambling dens and striptease shows. These, and dozens of other attractions, had their existence within The Great World. It was a favourite rendezvous for Australian and British soldiers on leave in Singapore—some of whom were to see it later in less agreeable circumstances. Came the war, and the lights of The Great World went out.

We journeyed in trucks from Changi, where we had been imprisoned since the surrender, to our unknown destination in town. Standing erect, we had been so skilfully compressed into the trucks by our Japanese drivers that satisfactory sightseeing was not possible. The twenty miles were swiftly and recklessly covered, and with a crashing of gears we stopped in front of a large, iron-walled enclosure which to many of us seemed vaguely

113

familiar. It was The Great World—but without any sign of its former greatness.

A few grunts from a guard indicated that we were to make ourselves at home. I thought of the 'Deserted Village' as we walked along alleyways where once a jostling torrent of humanity had flowed.

We were left to ourselves to find somewhere to sleep. Merv. Rowan, Tom Carroll, 'Hock' Mohr and myself settled for a former beauty salon, complete with plate glass windows, glass showcases, shelves and fittings. The other men—some 200 in all—made themselves comfortable in what had been beer gardens, coffee shops, theatres and a host of other deserted premises.

Soon the dead world came to life. We lacked beds, and carried all our possessions on our backs, but from the odd materials left behind by the previous occupiers an amazing variety of sleeping arrangements began to appear. We four slept in showcases until we were able to manufacture more comfortable substitutes from old wooden frames and camouflage tape.

Some of the prisoners who had some Malayan currency were amazed to find it was still legal tender in the city. We made this discovery when small Chinese boys appeared at gaps in the high iron fence offering cigarettes, bread and other items for sale. In no time each gap in the fence became a thriving trading centre. Men who had burnt their money upon capitulation began to sell what saleable possessions they had.

Our pleasure at our sudden change of circumstances was terminated suddenly by the appearance of Japanese guards who beat up any man caught trading, and meted out even harsher treatment to the courageous little Chinese boys who had eased our hunger for the first time since the capitulation. Time and again, small boys were caught and mercilessly beaten, but next day they would be back with their wares. Finally the Japanese, after hanging them by the feet for several hours, shaved a furrow down each offender's head—for future recognition. The wily boys, however, usually completed the haircut, and after a time the number of bald-headed boys in the vicinity of The Great World was remarkable.

After a day's settling-in, we discovered that our world was now a prison indeed—high galvanised-iron walls, topped with barbed wire, surrounded the camp, and a guard-house containing some twenty Japanese stood at the main entrance. Next day we were marshalled into groups and taken to work. The group of men detailed to work on the docks became known as the 'Wharf Party'; the other groups, including the one I was in, had no specific names, but went to toil daily at one of the many warehouses around town, including the British–American Tobacco Company's warehouse, Nestlé House, and several dumps which were our main centres.

Our first day's work proved more agreeable than we had expected. The march of about two miles through the streets under guard was a humiliating experience, repeated twice daily thereafter, although the native population, with its male members of working age notably absent, usually regarded us in sympathetic silence. Japanese guard-houses every half-mile or so were constant danger points, as failure to salute them with an 'eyes right' invariably resulted in the offenders being kicked or having their faces slapped.

We were mainly employed in shifting or stacking cases of tobacco and food, and loading and unloading trucks. It was during this daily routine at the British–American Tobacco Company's warehouse, which bore the scars of Japanese bombing, that we first met Sergeant Tassero.

Tassero held sway over all the warehouses and dumps in the area, where for the ensuing six months we were to spend most of our days. To do him justice, Tassero was not a bad man; by comparison with most of his compatriots he was an angel. He was tall and thin with a small head and prominent teeth, and he smiled often. He spoke in a high-pitched, squeaky voice but, clad in his uniform complete with jackboots and sword, he possessed a certain dignity. He had a mania for motorbikes and had acquired three or four for his personal use, only to lose

115

them one by one as his superior discovered their existence. In his quarters at the food dump he had also amassed a large collection of children's toys destined, he hoped, for the eventual delight of his offspring in Nippon. He possessed a sense of humour and I know of no prisoner of war—despite the continual provocation we gave him—who suffered any serious harm at his hands. Unfortunately Tassero was the only one of this species I ever encountered.

His three immediate subordinates were very different. Cymogie ('Smudgy' to us) was a repulsive, pockmarked little ferret of a man who resented Tassero's humanity and who usually instigated most of the searches for contraband among the prisoners. Sikista, a black-bearded Japanese who ruled Nestlé House, combined sadism with a natural appetite for causing trouble. If he could not find human victims he settled for monkeys, fowls or insects. King-jo could have been the village idiot back home in Japan. He possessed unusual strength and because of his inordinate vanity we often kidded him into performing many heavy tasks originally intended for the prisoners. The other dozen or so guards were a nondescript collection with one common attribute—a desire to hurt, humble and humiliate.

Under the eyes of this unsavoury crew of Japanese privates, our years of labour for Hirohito began. Our first job was to sort out truckloads of tinned foods which came in convoys from the various British Army dumps around the island—eventually destined for Japan. As we worked, we gorged. Taking turns at keeping the guards under observation, the daily work parties rotated through numerous courses of forbidden food. After a while the great difficulty was the disposal of evidence. This evidence gradually accumulated to an alarming extent under nearby stacks of food not being worked on at the time.

The day came when these stacks had to be removed and the exposure of the heaps of empty tins was unavoidable. The guards scratched their heads and gradually light dawned. That night as we lined up to go home we were suddenly pounced upon and searched. Men stood stiffly to attention. Joe hoped they would not locate the two tins of bully beef concealed in his underpants. Bill did not mind them taking the tins of milk out of his haversack, but felt pretty confident about the tins of tobacco strapped under his armpits. The guards went from man to man turning out pockets and upending haversacks. Soon a veritable mountain of tins appeared as the guards heaped the spoils in front of us. Tassero, supervising the operation, stood like a stunned plover, with his mouth open, but I think his sense of humour got the better of him as, after administering a half-hearted slap per man, he handed back one tin of milk between three of us, and sent us away. Searches became regular features of our lives, and Japanese vigilance around the dumps was redoubled.

While some men worked among food, others worked in the tobacco warehouses which contained the entire reserve of cigarettes and tobacco in Singapore. To smoke-starved men this was a labour of love. Scrounging originally for our personal requirements, we soon became aware that cigarettes had largely replaced money as a medium of exchange among the civilian population.

With the arrival of the Japanese, English and American cigarettes had disappeared from the legitimate market. Prisoners of war now assumed the role of suppliers to the civilian market, as they were the only non-Japanese link with the source. As we marched back to The Great World in the first days of our employment, we made tentative moves to barter with the Chinese. With each successive day, however, we and the Chinese became bolder.

The Japanese issued threats and warnings against any form of communication with the inhabitants of Singapore but, with two guards to 100 men, they had no chance of coping with the avalanche of humanity which swept alongside the homeward-bound column of POWs each night. Cigarettes furtively slipped out of pockets were grabbed by eager Chinese who in return gave bread, fruit and other edibles.

Life back in The Great World became almost pleasant. We accumulated stores of tobacco and food in secret hiding places.

Then we turned to seeking mental food as well. Books were brought in by parties working near private homes in Singapore and were exchanged for food. Most of the books were classics or educational—Lawrence's *Seven Pillars of Wisdom*, Homer's *Odyssey*, Virgil's *Aeneid* and Boccaccio's *Decameron* were only a few of the legacies inherited from our intellectual past. Boredom supplied the spur. The shearer, the drover, the bank clerk and the miner found new worlds in The Great World, ones that their peacetime occupations would never have offered.

The electrical fittings in the camp were soon restored by electricians in our ranks. The Japanese raised no objection apart from insisting on 'lights out' at nine o'clock each night. Resourceful hands soon fashioned immersion heaters, cookers, toasters and other electrical gadgets, until a stage was reached when the Japanese would have been staggered by the amount of power being consumed by the camp. Apparently they never bothered to read any meters, as jugs boiled and kettles simmered without any protest.

Night after night inquisitive guards poked through our quarters but only the most innocent of objects were ever conspicuous. Occasionally a photo of a girl might attract attention.

'Wifu?'

'Yes.'

'Baby?'

'Yes, ten.'

'*Jhoto*.' (Good)

The guard would then leave.

Many men could not sleep. After lights out they would sit around in groups in the darkness.

Every night when lights went out
The war was fought anew,
Fantastic rumours ran about,
And sleep was hard to woo.

A well-dressed Tamil had seen General Wavell in Singapore yesterday disguised as a rickshaw boy! If the Tamil or Chinese was well-dressed, additional credence was attributed to the current rumour.

A concert party was formed and the Globe opened its season. The players included a ballet complete with the daintiest of costumes. 'Stinky' McGeikie played the part of 'Mo' to perfection. The villainous 'squire' and the endangered 'virgin' trod the boards clad in appropriate garments. Camp technicians produced suitable lighting effects and POW artists provided the decor. We were amused and we were entertained. The virtue of some of the 'ballet girls' was jeopardised by the gullibility of some of our guards, until the removal of skilfully applied make-up revealed Smithy of the Wharf Party or Jones the greasy cook.

Compared with the prisoners at Changi, Bukit Timah, and other camps on the island, we were living like kings. However, our standard of living was entirely the result of our own enterprise, purchased at the risk of bashings, torture and, if the Japanese were so inclined, death itself.

The tins in which the camp rice was served resembled closely the tins usually placed around the camp at night as urinals. A particularly violent disturbance at one of the urinals one night involved Gunner Sykes, the heavyweight boxing representative of the 2/10th Field Regiment. Vic Sykes had ambled out on his nightly errand. In the process he was suddenly assailed by a young Japanese guard and savagely clubbed with a rifle butt.

'*Meshi* (food) tin! *Meshi* tin!' screamed the infuriated guard as he beat the astonished Sykes. Bruised and battered, the victim eventually escaped and reported the incident to the Australian camp commandant, Major Schneider. A conference with the Japanese interpreter disclosed that the guard—newly arrived in the camp—had thought that Gunner Sykes was polluting one of the prisoners' food vessels and had administered the punishment in the interests of Vic's fellow POWs.

Meantime our days were occupied under Tassero's surveillance. Occasionally we conversed with Japanese who were friendly towards us. A typical conversation, in a medium

composed of a mixture of Japanese, English and vigorous ges-
ticulations, went something like this:

Japanese: '*Nippon skorki* (aeroplanes) *Gorshu* (Australia) boom! boom!'
Aussie: 'Bullshit.'
Japanese: '*Nippon* Americano Navy boom! boom!'
Aussie: 'Yeah!'
Japanese: '*Nippon* English Navy boom! boom!'
Aussie: '*Nippon* Swiss Navy boom! boom?'
Japanese: '*Hai* (yes), Nippon Swiss Navy boom! boom!—all sunk.'

One of our early jobs under Tassero was to sort out old clothing and boots salvaged from the battlefield. Bloodstained jackets
and trousers were sorted out for laundering and ultimate reissue
to troops. The Japanese were most economical. For three weeks
a party of POWs sorted out sandboots, the standard footwear
of the Japanese jungle fighters. These were fastened on the foot
by means of three clips sewn on the back of the boot. For three
weeks the busy prisoners systematically ripped off the clips as
they worked.

As we worked we scrounged. Despite regular searches, vast
quantities of tobacco and food parted company from Tassero
each day. Various techniques were perfected. Some prisoners
favoured the cautious body-clinging forms of theft. Gunner
Parsons and others tried a bolder approach. With a case of
cigarettes on his shoulder, Stan Parsons brazenly strode out
of the door of the warehouse, saluting Sergeant Tassero as he
passed. Tassero acknowledged the salute, but ignored the case
of cigarettes which soon found its way back to The Great World
in small consignments.

The nightly mobile markets continued to operate as we
marched homewards, but the Japanese determined to crush the
trade. One afternoon a Chinese padded alongside the column
holding in his arms a luscious pawpaw. I bargained with him
at a distance of twenty feet. Finally he agreed to part with his
pawpaw for three packets of Players. He rushed across the road
and took my cigarettes but before I could grasp the pawpaw the

hands of the guard intercepted the fruit. As the Chinese fled with his Players the Japanese hurled the pawpaw with unerring aim and the last I saw of my customer was his head dripping with yellow pulp and black seeds as he ran up a side street.

Other encounters lacked the same humour. The pregnant Malay woman who was kicked in the stomach for trading a bunch of bananas for cigarettes most certainly paid a bitter price for disobeying the conquerors.

We stole food because we were hungry. In time thieving became a science.

'Red Light!' At the sound of this phrase lips were wiped, empty tins concealed, and expressions adjusted.

One of our fellow prisoners (known as 'Tich' or 'Mr Fourex') was a continual source of amusement and terror to his comrades. Tich (from the 2/26th Battalion) was a short soldier with a large head and the living image of a Brisbane identity who used to advertise a famous brand of Brisbane beer—Fourex. He was a good soldier and, like any POW, could not resist scrounging but unfortunately he could not help an unconscious exhibition of guilt. If Tich had concealed on his person a packet of cigarettes, his rolling eyes and bobbing head drew Japanese attention to him like a magnet and he was constantly caught and bashed. Unfortunately he also unwittingly attracted attention to his more subtle comrades. 'Cripes, here comes Tich, he's a moral to draw the crabs', was the inevitable reaction to his approach to any company.

During one memorable search, Tich stood to attention with two tins of bully beef balanced on his head beneath an English pith helmet. An angry guard had already extracted a great quantity of tobacco and foodstuffs from his pockets and haversack. The guard stood back and planted a well-directed punch on Tich's jaw. To his amazement, Tich's hat fell off and the two tins of bully beef clattered to the floor.

As usual this search yielded a prodigious quantity of loot. After the customary kicking and slapping, we were allowed to go home. To my astonishment, after entering the gates of The

Great World an even greater quantity of loot was disgorged by the previously searched men.

Finally the Japanese commandant of The Great World gave up all hope of abolishing trade with the locals and, as a compromise, allowed a certain number of them to enter the camp each night. He erected a long counter in front of the guardhouse and decreed that all POWs could legally spend their wages there. Our wages were ten cents a day! However, each night, every man in the camp spent something like three dollars. It seemed odd to us that the Japanese could each day witness, without comment, the spectacle of their prisoners spending more money than they earned in a fortnight. And not only that. Had they inspected the baskets of the fruit and bread merchants as they left the camp they would have been horrified.

The Chinese accepted any article whatever from the prisoners. Accordingly, in their baskets went revolvers, ammunition and knives. I even saw a small aeroplane wheel traded one day. No doubt these useful commodities found their way to the guerrillas. A cautious type myself, I marvelled at the courage of some of my fellow POWs and of the Chinese, for detection of any of these articles meant sudden death—and everyone knew it.

As time went by, many of the advantages of being in The Great World vanished. Scrounging became a crime for which the Japanese contrived more stringent penalties. When Sikista caught Garvie Ferrar stealing a tin of condensed milk, he had him tied up at the high school (Japanese headquarters) and subjected him to constant torture for two days. Each morning the Japanese interpreter emptied the ashtrays in his face, spat on him, and burnt his stomach with cigarette butts. Dozens of methods designed to render a person penitent were applied, but Garvie took them all. Finally they half-drowned him in a horse trough. After that the interpreter grudgingly shook hands with him and let him go.

Soon our work at the tobacco warehouse petered out. Before it did, however, I shared one unusual experience with Gunner

Merv Rowan. On this particular day we approached the guard on the gate and, assuming imbecilic expressions, made gestures as if cleaning our teeth and pointed towards the town which was only 100 yards away. The guard nodded patronisingly and away we went.

We passed many Japanese soldiers and officers in the street but as long as we saluted them all, they showed no curiosity in two prisoners wandering at large. This attitude seemed typical throughout. A Japanese who had no control over POWs showed little interest in what they did. Merv and I made our way into an empty Malay beer shop where we flashed a packet of cigarettes with the question: '*Brapa?*' (How much?) The shopkeeper pointed to a door at the end of the shop and we entered and laid our cigarettes on a table, receiving half-a-dollar for each packet. With the proceeds we bought a couple of bottles of beer and sat down to drink. After a few bottles, several locals entered and before long we found ourselves half-drunk. In our state of intoxication, we were planning to retake the island. In fact we had it all sewn up when the locals began to show alarm and left in a hurry. On noticing the time, we sobered up as if by magic and wondered how we would explain our two hours' absence to the guard. But somehow or other we rejoined the working party without mishap.

Merv Rowan immediately got himself into a party working in Nestlé House—his reason being that in Nestlé House were stored some cases of fine Pommery—and he had decided another little drink would not do him any harm. He got his bottle of Pommery and later, as he leaned against a wall to support himself, some unusually sympathetic Japanese diagnosed his incapacity as malaria and relieved him from further work.

I was placed in charge of a party of ten men and detailed to move stacks of lumber. While so engaged I became very sleepy and lay down behind a stack for a short nap. I awoke to a rude shaking by one of the party, Stan Parsons, who told me the others had gone back to camp. Walking along with Stan, I was fully prepared for some dire punishment at the first guard-house but a suitable 'eyes right' plus a shout of malaria from Stan carried us past most of the guard-houses. To finish the day we hired a rickshaw and rode the rest of the way in state. At the entrance to the camp I assumed an attitude of acute illness, and with much talk of malaria from Parsons we stumbled in to safety.

On several occasions a party left the camp to work at the brewery. It was amazing the number of malaria cases that returned from such jobs!

After we had been prisoners for six months, work became something of a lottery. Most of the prisoners were sent to the wharf but several small parties were made up each day and taken to work at all manner of odd places. Selection for these parties depended upon one's position in the ranks and the whim of the Japanese in charge. One day it might be the pineapple factory in Johore Bahru, another day it might be one of the hundreds of warehouses along the evil-smelling canal.

On one such occasion a party was taken to cut grass near Tengah aerodrome and bale it for horse fodder. While cutting the grass we found the skeleton of an Australian soldier, his hands bound behind his back with signal wire. A further search revealed three shallow graves in a nearby rubber plantation, beside a position that had been held by the 2/15th Field Regiment. Only one of the bodies wore an identity disc. A great stack of empty charge cases by the position told its own story.

While on another of these working parties we came across seven or eight Australian Bren carriers. They were drawn up in a circle and had been burnt out. Bones still remained within them and there was every indication that there had been an heroic fight to the finish by the men who manned them. On these out-of-the-ordinary working parties we continually stumbled across lonely graves of British and Australian soldiers, many of them bearing fresh flowers laid by the staunch Japanese-hating Chinese. The only solace for such moving discoveries was that an infinitely greater number of 'totem poles' (the

Japanese method marking the graves of their dead) were to be seen. Around Bukit Timah particularly, the Japanese death toll seemed to have been very heavy.

Working parties such as these, however, were exceptions to the rule. We were now 'wharfies' most of the time and our life out of The Great World was tied up with ships and trains. Rubber, tin, rice and the other sources of Malaya's wealth, which the Japanese were pouring into the hold of their ships, flowed in a never-ending stream to the docks. It was on the wharf that we first met the 'finish, go home' trick. A train consisting of twelve trucks, each containing 200 bags of rice, would be presented to us with the command 'Finish, go home'. Working flat out we might be home by four o'clock. Next day the train would consist of sixteen trucks. 'Finish, go home' still applied. The same tactics were employed on the ships. The result was that the Japanese cunningly ascertained the maximum effort of which we were capable and then extracted it from us over the minimum time. Again and again we were to fall for this ruse in Singapore, Thailand and Japan.

When a convoy arrived, work was heavy and constant, with no mechanical aids to help us. Whether the cargo was bags of rice, salt, sugar or cement, the rule was one man one bag, irrespective of the size of the man. Trolleys were unheard of— the heavy bags were lumbered into the godowns and stacked by manpower. The godowns lining the dockside contained an infinite variety of goods, ranging from lipstick to aeroplanes. Many had been destroyed by Japanese bombing but the others remained a constant temptation to enterprising prisoners of war.

The whole of the dock area was wired in and guarded by the dreaded Kempei-Tai guards. Any pilferer discovered by these gentry was usually not fit to scrounge for a long time. Nevertheless, each night cartons of lipstick, sewing machine needles, photographic plates and a host of other commodities went back to The Great World on the bodies of POWs. These goods brought fantastic prices from the Chinese and many considered the rewards to be worth the risk.

As time went on, however, searches became more thorough until the stage was reached when the guards forced prisoners to drop their trousers and even combed their hair for sewing machines needles.

One day two inquisitive prisoners strayed from their gang into an empty godown and to their delight unearthed a bottle of crème de menthe which they drank. In the midst of this operation they were suddenly pounced on by a 'Black Triangle' guard with his bayonet ready for action. Quick as a flash one of the men poured some of the precious liquid on his hands and began to rub it assiduously into his hair. The guard, nonplussed as he watched this strange proceeding, finally took off his cap (all Japanese soldiers kept their heads shaved) and pointed to his own skull. The prisoners nodded vigorously and by signs conveyed the impression that his hair would sprout instantly under such treatment. The three parted amicably, the Australians concealing their relief and the Japanese guard smothering his head with crème de menthe.

In another godown where regular working parties toiled, the Japanese custodian had a habit of laying baits for the unwary in the form of tins of food. One day he placed a tin of condensed milk on a box in an inconspicuous corner and waited hopefully. Dinner time arrived and the tin of milk remained unmoved. Expressing amazement and pleasure, the Japanese, quite unaware of the consumption of at least a case of milk taken quietly from elsewhere in the stack, lined up the prisoners and presented them with a tin of milk between five men for honesty. Then, assailed by some misgiving, he picked up his tin of milk, to find it empty with a neat hole drilled in the bottom!

The same Japanese guard decided one day to demonstrate his knowledge of the crafty methods employed by Australians to appropriate the Emperor's property. The particular trick he intended demonstrating was in fact one of the least spectacular in the prisoners' repertoire. Whenever a suitable object presented itself for scrounging, the scrounger would casually throw his hat on top of it as he passed. Later he would return and just as casually retrieve the hat along with the tin of food beneath it. Our Japanese guard ostentatiously placed a tin of bully beef on a box then, in the Australian manner, he walked by, throwing his cap over the tin as he passed. When he turned and retrieved his hat he was thunderstruck to find that the tin was not under it. During the instant his back was turned, a prisoner with a sense of humour had deftly removed the tin. Incidents such as these occurred in the various parties throughout our period of employment.

Another group of Australians from The Great World operated as a transport unit, even bringing their trucks back at night. These men were master scroungers—each truck was fitted with false petrol tanks and a false bottom. When they cooperated with other workers, their hauls were spectacular.

During our wharf labouring days many incidents not directly affecting ourselves did not pass unnoticed. There was the case of a murdered Japanese truck driver. As a reprisal, seven or eight local civilians were publicly beheaded in front of the Cathay building (Singapore's only skyscraper) and their heads placed in prominent positions round the town. One of the heads was placed on the gate of the railway station, past which many of our working parties marched on their way to work. The head sat on a board for a week with signs in several languages stating the alleged reason for the execution, together with the warning: 'There is more room on the board'. Some of the less reverent POWs bade the head 'good morning' as they passed.

Ships taking Japanese repatriates home called at Singapore. It made us homesick to see the Europeanised Japanese walking about in their English and American suits.

Later still, we helped unload rubber from a badly holed German raider, the *Regenberg*. An English-speaking German handed us cigarettes and expressed sympathy as we worked our night shifts near his ship. It was good to see white men walking free in the midst of our Asian slave drivers, even though they were Germans. It was still more pleasant for the men who watched a burly German flatten one arrogant Japanese guard who attempted to carry out his bullying tactics on board the German ship.

A daily sight in the dockyard was that of a dozen-or-so men each standing on one leg and balancing a bucket of water on his head. If the water spilled, the offender would be beaten on the shins with batons. This meant the spilling of more water and more bashing—a fine sport for the Japanese and Sikh guards. One day I witnessed the torture of some Chinese boys who had been caught stealing rice. Sikh guards (probably the same police who were employed formerly by the British) seized the unfortunate boys and, after pumping water into their stomachs from a fire hydrant, beat them on their stomachs with batons. Some of the boys died as a result.

Another day, as we worked on a shipload of cement, we saw a submarine undergoing trials in the harbour. Suddenly, with a great swishing of water and a sharp explosion, under she went. At the time we did not realise she had gone under for good. Our first indication that something was amiss came at dinner time when we were ordered to fall in and march to the guard-house. Prior to this, Gunner Petullo had salvaged the gyro-compass from an American fighter plane crated on the wharf. He had the compass in his pocket as we marched off and other members of the party had sabotaged other parts of the aircraft for good measure. Reaching the guard-house we were searched with more than usual care. As the search commenced men began jettisoning their loot in the gutter behind us. However, with characteristic single-mindedness the Japanese concentrated this time on written material. Any books found were confiscated. Then we learned that the submarine had been sabotaged. To our amazement the pile of food, bicycle chains, lipstick, razor blades and other articles lying in the gutter behind us was ignored by the Japanese as they marched off again.

Down at the docks there were many other efforts at sabotage. Men in the holds of ships systematically punctured four-gallon tins of various fluids destined for the Japanese troops. Others urinated in tins of fruit juice, topped up 44-gallon drums of petrol and then screwed down the caps so that the drums would burst at the slightest increase in temperature. These and many other acts gave us a feeling that our usefulness to our country had not entirely disappeared.

Throughout our imprisonment under Nippon, the Japanese never ceased reminding us that we were the sons of convicts— an indication of the Japanese version of Australian history as taught in their schools.

As we marched to and fro each day through the ever-saddening city, we often met contingents of Gurkhas. Japanese or no, the Gurkhas gave us the 'eyes right' each time we passed, and we returned their salute. No amount of Japanese cursing and raving ever prevented that exchange of courtesy. We had known the smiling little hillmen as free brothers-in-arms and we were proud to acknowledge them as brothers-in-captivity.

Our knowledge of the Japanese language increased slowly. '*Shigoto*' meant work; '*Tucsan shigoto*' meant plenty work. Their knowledge of English comprised the word 'Speedo' and 'Finish, go home'.

The tolerance shown towards us in the early months began to disappear. First, the counter outside the guard-house was closed, probably because a Chinese civilian had shot dead a Japanese guard outside the camp a few days earlier.

Then word came through that we were to move to River Valley Road, a camp that we knew was less than half-a-mile from The Great World. We were soon to learn many things about River Valley Road.

To me, The Great World was a merciful introduction to the dark days which followed. While my fellow prisoners of war elsewhere had embarked upon their purgatory of hunger and worse, I had stored my frame with vitamins in preparation for what I did not know was coming. I had seen Stan Parsons devour a large tin of Lactogen at one sitting, and myself and others had done the same.

The pages of experience were now to be filled with incidents the like of which I could never have dreamt.

129

17

The embankment at Wampo

I N March 1943, 500 Australian prisoners of war in 'T' Battalion of D Force arrived at Bampong in Thailand. They had travelled by train from Singapore, a five-day journey in enclosed steel rice vans. From Bampong they were taken in flat-top carriages over the newly constructed section of the Burma–Thailand railway which ended at Kanburi (now Kanchanaburi).

There our guards abruptly left us and no other Japanese in the area showed the slightest interest in us. 'I don't think the bastards can feed us any more', my mate Stan Parsons said. 'They've just dumped us here to fend for ourselves.'

Accordingly we built rough bush shelters and began trading our few possessions with the local Thais for eggs, bananas and coffee. Life became one long feast.

At the end of a week our illusion of freedom was shattered by the arrival of a batch of abusive, brutal guards from whom we learnt that our week of freedom had been the result of a mistake.

We were quickly herded together, put into trucks and driven north and west into the mountains, away from human habitation and what went with it.

In a swirl of dust, the convoy passed a gang of convicts, legs chained as they worked under the guns of the Japanese guards.

We passed a few scattered settlements encircled by high

bamboo stockades to keep out tigers and other wild animals, and then began a steep ascent through massive clumps of bamboo. In the trees between the clumps, colonies of monkeys shrieked and gibbered at the passing trucks.

A drab attap-roofed camp loomed ahead and soon we entered the gates of Tarsau POW camp. A gaunt group of human beings plodded by in the opposite direction without greeting or comment. Most were like skeletons. Their green Dutch uniforms were in rags, blood ran down their legs and they were mottled with filthy sores. One man limped along carrying his testicles which were the size of footballs.

We slept overnight at Tarsau and in the morning walked ten miles south to our first job on the railway. We erected tents in a stony creek bed and then began building a low embankment across a flat stretch of country above the river. The tents were overcrowded and the rice sour but no one was greatly dismayed by his first acquaintance with railway work.

Lieutenant Sumi, the Japanese engineer in charge of the job, was a clear-faced, serious man who set reasonable tasks and discouraged his men from bashing us. He spoke a little English. At the end of each day he allowed us to swim in the river.

Within two weeks the embankment was finished and Sumi was delighted.

'*Gorshu* (Australia) plenty good workers', he said. '*Nippon* give big party. All men *tucsan meshi* (cut bamboo). Tonight make big fire.'

Later that day Sumi's engineers dynamited the river and we swam to retrieve hundreds of stunned fish which floated to the surface. Sumi also arranged a concert and when night came the farewell party began beneath the stars.

The Japanese sat in a group on one side of the great bonfire and the Australians formed up on the other. Sumi, who fancied himself as a singer and conductor, ordered the concert to begin—the Australians to sing first.

The prisoners obeyed with 'Waltzing Matilda', followed by 'God Save the King'. The Japanese applauded politely.

Sumi's choir then sang and the Australians clapped. The party went smoothly until one of the prisoners stood and sang 'My Blue Heaven'. Sumi delightedly praised the man for singing a Japanese song, and to prove his point ordered his engineers to sing the song in Japanese.

'That's not a Jap song', someone scoffed. 'It's like all the other things you copy from us.'

'English copy from Japanese', Sumi retorted, showing signs of displeasure.

The former friendly spirit began to deteriorate as the party progressed. When the Japanese choir started to sing, 'She'll Be Coming Round the Mountain', Parsons turned to me. 'Here we go again. I'll bet someone picks Sumi up on this one.'

My attention was elsewhere as I appreciatively sniffed the odour of fresh fish frying over makeshift ovens.

There was a pause after the Japanese had finished singing, and then spontaneously some 500 voices began bellowing the Australian version:

They'll be flyin' in formation when they come,
They'll be flyin' in formation when they come,
They'll be flyin' in formation, they'll be flyin' in formation,
They'll be flyin' in formation when they come.

Joining in the deafening chorus, I realised with astonishment that the whole act, although completely unpremeditated, had been as unanimous as if it had been the will of one individual.

They'll be droppin' thousand-pounders when they come,
They'll be droppin' thousand-pounders when they come,
They'll be droppin' thousand-pounders, they'll be droppin' thousand-pounders,
They'll be droppin' thousand-pounders when they come.

Silence fell like an iron lid over the creek bed as Sumi translated to his men the words the Australians had sung. Then the lid slowly lifted under the swelling pressure of Japanese anger.

Sumi snatched a bamboo pole from the fire and started

belting the prisoners close to him. His men quickly followed his example and the party disintegrated in uproar. Scrambling beyond the perimeter of the fire's glow, the prisoners fled to their tents while the Japanese returned to eat what fish they could. The rest they threw into the river.

Fumbling in the dark for my bed, I heard Parsons's voice raised in lament. 'The silly cows could at least have left that song until after we'd had our fish.'

The following morning Lieutenant Sumi handed over his prisoners to a batch of guards who had arrived to herd them further south. Tents were packed and the column of prisoners started off along a narrow jungle track between the river and a nearby parallel mountain. Tremendous clumps of bamboo arched above them, screening the sky and hiding all else but the track ahead.

We had been walking all day—strung out along the jungle track like a winding column of ants. Towards evening a series of sudden dull explosions ripped along a hidden ridge to the left and seconds later the insubstantial bamboo canopy above was smashed by a hail of rocks and stones. Instinctively some men went to ground. Others, like Parsons and me, were too weary to care. The track ended in a clearing, beyond the edge of which a huddle of attap roofs was visible.

Crossing the clearing we stared up at a thin scar gouged by dynamite along the mountain side. Dust and smoke whisked up by the recent explosion hung in small clouds along its bare rocky route, ending where the mountain met the river. At the junction, a towering mound of freshly dry earth marked the site of a mighty embankment.

'Jesus!' Parsons said. 'I don't like the look of that. Reminds me of the bloody Pyramids.'

An evilly handsome Japanese, known to British soldiers already in the camp as the 'Black Prince' welcomed the incoming prisoners by bashing up half-a-dozen men just to show who was who. His nickname was promptly amended to the 'Black Bastard' by the Australians.

Slim Kirk, Parsons and I moved into a tent with twenty other men. On the following day we were routed out in the darkness before dawn and, after a cup of watery rice per man, herded up to the embankment. Through an interpreter, the Black Bastard announced that the embankment had to be finished in two weeks. The line had already been laid to the other side of the spur and, whatever the cost, it would be extended across the embankment at the end of a fortnight. On the job, he divided the prisoners into groups of four—a shovel man, a pick man, and two men carrying a stretcher improvised from a rice bag and two bamboo poles.

'So all we have to do each day', Parsons said,' is dig a grave and carry the dirt up on top of that flamin' mountain.'

I nodded towards a guard busy belabouring four Australians with a pick handle. 'That's right, and you'd better start digging or we'll have the moron on us next.'

'I can understand why they brought us here', Slim Kirk said as he and I trudged up the steep slope with a stretcher load of earth. 'Did you ever see a filthier camp in your life? Or men nearer to skeletons than those Pommies? They've had a tough trot', Slim continued. 'Specially all those jokers with beri-beri. Some of 'em have testicles as big as your head. Others have legs and arms like balloons. Makes a man sick to look at 'em.'

He grunted as his feet went from under him on the slippery slope. 'Don't think many of them will see the line out.'

'We're going to be battling ourselves', I said. 'We have to shift something like three cubic metres of earth each shift. That's going to take some doing on the lousy scrap of tucker we're getting.'

At the top of the embankment we gained a short rest by prolonging the emptying of the stretcher. After a brief pause to look out over the tops of the bamboo we started the descent. Below, the scene resembled a disturbed ants' nest, with long lines of men trudging backwards and forwards carrying dirt. A guard came out of the darkness and punched Slim behind the ear, hastening our return for more earth.

One day was the same as another. From the dark before dawn

until long after the sun went down, weary legs followed the same paths up and down the wall-like embankment. At night men stumbled into rain-sodden tents and slept where they fell. A strange silence born of exhaustion came upon the five hundred, and soon the number itself began to shrink. Stinking, makeshift hospital tents filled rapidly with dysentery and malaria cases, and the Black Bastard administered medicine with a bamboo pole.

'I think I must be dead and in hell.' Parsons was on the night shift and I was with him. It was the last night shift of the job and before we had left camp that night the Black Bastard had decreed that every man would continue working until the job was finished, no matter how long it took.

'They'll soon weed us out at this rate', Parsons continued. 'Working like a horse on nothing but sour rice and watery peanut soup. My stomach feels as if my throat's cut.'

We had carried a stretcher of dirt to the top of the embankment and had merged with the shadows to regain our breath. Parsons pointed down. 'Have a look at that. Ever seen anything more like a lunatic's nightmare?'

Dozens of bamboo fires were burning on a wide flat at the foot of the embankment. The leaping flames cast grotesque, dancing shadows all over the hole-studded ground and on it the sweating bodies of men gleamed as they moved mechanically like polished robots. Snarling Japanese *hanchos* (bosses) wearing white, mushroom-shaped helmets darted among the toiling prisoners, flogging them to greater efforts.

Silhouetted against the glare of a fire an Australian stood on a boulder holding a large rock above his head. He was being punished for working too slowly. Near him two prisoners were chasing each other endlessly around a tree.

'We'd better get going', I said. 'The pick and shovel men might get landed for standing around.'

Halfway down the hill Parsons, at the leading end of the stretcher, stopped and turned. 'Too late. Look.'

I looked. Slim Kirk, our shovel man, with a guard standing

over him, was trying to roll a large rock up the embankment. Like Sisyphus, he would roll the stone up two feet, only to have it roll back three feet. The guard was enjoying himself and every now and then encouraged him by hitting him on the head with a heavy stick.

Back at the hole the pick man was receiving another form of punishment. Standing on one leg, he was holding a crowbar over his head while a tiny guard amused himself by burning him on the navel with a lighted cigarette. The night wore on and morning came, followed by a blistering hot day. By now men were dropping to the ground. When they failed to respond to such methods of resuscitation as beatings and applied cigarette ends, they were lugged back to camp. But work went on.

At midnight the embankment was completed and we carried Slim back to camp on a stretcher.

The Black Bastard allowed us to sleep throughout the following day. We were incapable of doing anything else. On the next day we began to walk north to another task.

Of the five hundred who had started work on the embankment, less than four hundred were fit to walk. At least those we left behind were to be spared the horrors of our next job which came to be known as 'Hell Fire Pass'.

18

Japan after Burma and Thailand

THE first party of prisoners of war from the Burma–Thailand Railway to reach Japan was a force of 2250 men, including 1000 Australians, under Captain Reg Newton. They sailed in two ships from Singapore on 4 July 1944, and disembarked at Moji after a nightmare voyage of 70 days.

Among the prisoners on the *Rashin Maru* was WO2 Syd Barber of 8th Division Ammo Sub Park—a unit that supplied ammunition. He was one of four men who developed cardiac beri-beri on the voyage and had been kept alive by the self-sacrifice and dedication of Dr Hinder, one of the two medical officers on board. The treatment was a jar of Marmite and four ampoules of Thiamine which he had hoarded from the Railway. Syd Barber describes his arrival in Japan and his destination when the prisoners were lined up on the wharf, arbitrarily split into five groups and dispersed in different directions.

I was in a detachment which was sent to Seganoseki, near Moji, as a pool of forced labour to work in a metal refinery. It consisted entirely of Australians and part of the detachment was made up from the Tasmanian 2/40th Battalion from Timor, Navy crewmen from HMAS *Perth* and RAAF aircrew from Singapore, Java and Sumatra. The Tasmanians included some fellows from Mount Lyell whose knowledge of metals and mining was to prove invaluable. Our senior Australian officer was Lt Ron Williams, OC, Carrier

Platoon, 2/40th Battalion. He was accepted as Camp Commander by the Nips and we were pleased to have an Aussie as commander.

We had been issued with light shorts, singlets and other clothing of tropical weight and were now issued with clothing of a more substantial nature. We did not know then but Japan was about to experience one of its severest winters for many years. The clothing consisted of a kind of long cotton underwear, khaki jackets and trousers woven from twisted rice paper, a pair of Japanese rubber-soled shoes, a cap, and best of all, an American greatcoat, probably from Manila.

The camp was also much better than anything we had on the Railway. Long wooden huts were furnished with sleeping benches covered with *tatami* matting over a bamboo framework. These ran the full length of the hut and extended about seven feet out from the wall. The ultimate luxury was a sort of padded quilt for warmth. Main heating was provided by one charcoal fire in a terra-cotta pot about the size of a nine-inch flower pot. The charcoal ration was about a half-a-dozen pencil-size sticks per hut. Outside toilets were provided, with female labour to remove the waste products and clean the building. There were also outdoor ablution troughs and bamboo sticks for clothes lines, and the whole camp was enclosed by a high wooden fence.

We found the local Japanese civilians to be quite civil and reasonably friendly at first. Things were not all that pleasant for them at this stage of the War, and food was not over plentiful . . . Our fellows worked on two main activities in the refinery—'converters' and blast furnaces. There were four furnaces named Ichigoro, Nigoro, Sangoro and Yongoro. Yongoro was a bit 'sick' and it was my section's task to service it. The refinery worked on a gravity-feed system and ore, coke, limestone, scrap metal and *karami*, which seemed to be some kind of slag, was loaded into hoppers at the top of the hill from electric tram-type trucks operated by Koreans. We worked level with the top of the blast furnaces. Trucks moving on steel tracks were pushed by prisoners of war into tunnels, where Korean supervisors, working from a blackboard menu prepared by a Japanese engineer, would nominate three trucks of coke, one limestone, one *karami* or whatever was the brew for the day. During that winter when the maw of the furnace was exposed, there was a blast of intense heat and a glimpse of one of the suburbs of hell. In the tunnels we also worked up a sweat but in between we had to run the gauntlet through the icy wind back to the tunnel.

Sometimes Yongoro was very hungry, and then the work was

hard, and Nip tempers short. At others, Yongoro was sick and had no appetite.

Then the Nips and prisoners of war all had a bludge, but this was not often. Our old section supervisor, a retired employee called up for the duration, was named Nagano (horse). When he came to collect his charges at the beginning of the shift, he was always delighted when he could tell us 'Yongoro byoki, taksan yasume!' (No. 4 furnace is sick. Plenty of rest.)

One of the most important establishments at the works was the Mud Factory. This was powered by an elderly horse which plodded round in a circle turning a great paddle in a large vat. This produced a special breed of mud used to seal off the slag outlets on the furnaces, dam molten slag and for a host of other tasks, all vital to the smooth running of the works.

By now Seganoseki was receiving regular visits from a family in Tinian in the Marianas. The Nips called them the *B-Nijukus*. We knew them as B-29s and their bombload consisted of a high proportion of small, Thermite incendiary bombs which rained down like confetti. The damage they did to small timber buildings can be imagined. However, one day we were paid a more ominous visit. Fighters. Short-range stuff. That meant that there must be an aircraft carrier close to the coast. This had a worse effect on Nip morale than any of the long-range, heavy bombing raids. To make matters worse they destroyed the Mud Factory, but fortunately did not hurt the old horse.

During raids there was a mild panic among the Koreans and a rush for the tunnels. Our brave shift boss, who was always boasting about his fine service in Manchuria, would head the stampede by a couple of lengths. It was a strange feeling to be barracking for the bombing crews—'That's the stuff, fellows! Plaster the joint! But please, not me or my mates. Not now that I have got this far!' Eventually, one of the raids hit the town's communal rice storage buildings, which were completely razed. After some negotiation we were allowed to have the damaged rice as a free addition to camp rations, and we had already learned in Thailand that even badly burnt rice makes a fair substitute for coffee.

We had to march through the town to the works each shift and you could sense the attitude of the civilians changing as the bombing program progressively hotted up. We understood. It was not hard to imagine the Australian reaction in a country town if the boot had been on the other foot: Damn them anyway! They started it!

Among the better know personalities in the camp at that time were the brothers Don and Dick Abbott and Eric Smith, all from the 2/20th Battalion, Doug Draper, Alex Ross, Johnnie Souter, Geoff Dewey, Bill Belford and Tom Young from RAAF squadrons and all aircrew except Draper. Don Abbott was very fond of the old Australian Bush ballads of Banjo Paterson, Adam Lindsay Gordon and their ilk and had written a few himself. Bill Belford was a good amateur boxer and, in Thailand, used to spar with another keen boxer named Tom Uren who was also in the camp. Their sparring was given up, on medical advice, when it was pointed out that an accidental blow or fall could seriously damage spleens already affected by repeated attacks of malaria. Both men had a lot of guts and offered only grudging obedience to the Nips. After the War, Bill Belford continued in his teaching profession and Tom Uren entered politics, eventually to become a Cabinet minister in the Whitlam and Hawke governments.

One of our problems in working on the blast furnaces was loss of salt through sweat, and there was none issued in our rations. We knew that furnace workers back home sucked salt tablets to replace this loss, so since sea-water was widely used in the works, we boiled this down on the little cast iron stove in the 'rest' hut. The brass containers we boiled it in turned a brilliant green, but it was the salt our bodies craved.

As we learned more about our jobs, the supervisors left more and more to the prisoners of war, and retired to the warm rest hut. When this happened, the blackboard menu was ignored and we stoked lots and lots of coke and limestone and very little else. When we came to Seganoseki there was one furnace, Yongoro, which was slightly sick, but after this kind of treatment, the time came when three were burnt out and the remaining one very sick. We liked to think of it as our contribution to their war effort.

The works were now in bad shape, and with the change in the fortunes of war, our days at Seganoseki were numbered. Late in June we moved to Omine. Looking back, the people of Seganoseki had been comparatively kindly and showed some concern for our fellows. Not so in Omine. To begin with , it was run by the Mitsui-Mitsubishi organisation, a kind of Japanese equivalent of the German Krupps. The staff were regimented and wore the triple diamond logo, now familiar in Australia, on their black miners' caps. We had been moved there from Seganoseki to provide labour in its coalmines. We were not impressed by the fact that we would be joining a camp of mixed nationalities: British from Singapore, Dutch from Java and Sumatra, and Canadians from the Winnipeg Fusiliers and Royal Rifles of Canada captured in Hong Kong. The only officers were Dutch and American, the senior being an American major. They seemed to spend most of their time playing cards, and to show little concern for their men. Ron Williams quietly took charge of all Australian affairs and the other officers seemed to be happy to be relieved of the worry, but soon everyone in the camp looked to him for leadership. We, of course, liked the arrangement.

The camp consisted of two-storeyed buildings made from the Japanese equivalent of wattle-and-daub, a bamboo framework covered with mud. Internal walls were a bamboo framework covered with rice-paper. The whole camp was again surrounded by a high wooden wall. A large bathhouse was furnished with a big double container of hot water, one section in which to remove the loose coaldust, and the other to really clean the body.

On entering the mine each man was issued with an electric lamp to clip on his cap, attached by a lead to a battery which was to be hooked on to his belt. The Nips believed in getting every last skerrick of coal, picking around outcropping rocks in the floor of the shaft and leaving the hollows to fill with water. Similarly, in the roof the coal would be picked out, leaving stalactites of limestone descending from the roof. Air was pumped into the shaft through a four-inch pipe which wound its way along the roof or floor. These were the obstacles we encountered until we became familiar with the traps and learned to always point our heads at what we wanted to see. Timbering to support the roof of the shaft was not as sturdy as that used in Australian mines, and when we were in the shaft we could always hear the grinding sound of the load shifting.

The sloping shaft leading down to the working galleries was just wide enough for a skip moving on iron tracks. Each skip had a rolled edging which extended outwards for about two inches. As the roof load shifted, the supporting timbers would bow inward until they were struck by the edge of the skips. To rectify this problem, the resourceful Koreans simply chopped a V out of the timber with an axe. Eventually the timber would be weak enough to break and a cave-in would result.

From about mid-1945, life followed a fairly monotonous pattern. We received news from the Koreans in the mines on the progress of the war, and spirits began to rise. We began to have concert parties, and spent off-duty time in other activities as in the early Changi days. One of these activities took the form of an art group and was run by Geoff Tyson, a member of the 2/40th Battalion, who had been a cartoonist on a Tasmanian newspaper. After the war he published a book of sketches which formed an excellent record of Omine in the closing months of the Pacific War.

Meanwhile, work in the mine went on. One of my best mates was badly beaten up by a shift boss using an iron goad in one of the most brutal, savage attacks I have seen. But Japanese morale was beginning to crumble. All available able-bodied men were overseas and only the very old, the very young and the infirm remained to defend the sacred soil.

19

Torpedoed

T HE movement of prisoners of war to Japan began in 1942 and continued until mid-1945, by which time some 35 000, including 2700 Australians, were spread in about 100 camps around the main islands of Japan.

Most of them had been transported in small cargo ships of 4000 to 6000 tons, and more often than not prisoners were jammed into holds already loaded with supplies such as rubber, hides, latex, bauxite and ingots of tin. The hardships, over-crowding, starvation and disease suffered by the POWs on these voyages were horrifying and there was always the threat of Allied submarines and aircraft.

Among the 10 853 prisoners of war lost at sea were 1515 Australians.

One batch of prisoners of war from the Burma–Thailand rail-way was the force of 2300 under Brigadier Varley which sailed from Singapore for Japan on 6 September 1944 in two ships, the *Rokyu Maru* and the *Kachidori Maru*. The ships never arrived. Gunner Kitch Loughnan of the 2/10th Field Regiment was aboard the *Rokyu Maru* and has recorded what happened.

On 13 September 1944, about five o'clock in the morning, we were awakened with a jolt. A torpedo went straight through the bow. Water came through the hold. We panicked for a while! Someone got up on top and told us we were sinking and to take things easy. That really shook us up! Dinny Morgan and I were jammed in the hold, but I eventually got out. I never saw Dinny again. I looked for him.

There were a lot of other ships sunk at the same time. Two tankers set all the water alight. Some men got into boats, but most had to jump over and swim. We thought the fire on top of the water would catch us up. I was one of the last to jump off. Pat Allan and Jim Kennedy were with me. Major Chalmers told us the ship was starting to list a good bit, and he thought we had better jump over. We kept swimming away from the flames. We never worried; Leo Chambers, Doc Savage and Jim Kennedy said, 'Don't worry, the Yanks will pick us up'.

The *Rokyu Maru* was a Japanese cargo ship transporting prisoners to Japan and not carrying cargo. The Americans thought it was taking cargo as the ship did not have any Red Cross signs on it saying prisoners were aboard. Our bad luck! Anyway, it was the Americans who sank us. They did not know, poor chaps.

Time went by and the Americans did not turn up. We were a long way east of our ship and it was still afloat. There were two or three Jap corvettes going around looking for submarines. The corvettes would go straight over the swimmers, never trying to miss them. Too bad if you were in the way, you were dead! All of a sudden one corvette was blown to pieces. I suppose it was about a quarter of a mile from us, but the percussion in the water started to affect us.

Then the other two corvettes started dropping depth charges. It was the depth charges that bugged us. They started to kill our fellows like fish. We began to hold our 'very sick' on bamboo. It was a shambles! [I] lifted Leo Chambers on to some bamboo for a rest.

About forty of us started to swim back to the ship, but only five of us made it—Doc Savage, Bill Webb, Clarrie Wilson, an English chap and myself. There have been many stories told about this, but WE WERE THE LAST OFF AND ON THE SHIP. I was buggered. We must have swum about three miles. I would never have made it but for Bill Webb, who kept waiting for me. We had nothing to hang on to, just had to keep swimming. All my mouth was bleeding and also between my legs. It was all caused by pellagra, and the salt water did not help! I had a job to pull myself on to the ship's ladder. If I had had any sense I would have swum around the ship and on to the top of the deck. Anyhow, I eventually pulled myself up and got on

144

to the deck and lay there. Bill Webb and the other chaps scrounged around and got a tin of dried fish, a can of water and a bottle of brandy. Also, we found four hatch boards which we tied together, without much success. They kept on coming apart. We tried to lift Clarrie Wilson on to the boards, as he was sick.

We did not have time to try to release the lifeboat which was hanging off the ship. The ship was going down and we just had time to move away. We swam away from the *Rokyu Maru* a little way as she gave a plunge and sank near us. Planks, drums and all kinds of things kept on coming up, but we were never hit by anything or sucked down with the ship. A miracle!

I think that was the only time we sort of gave in. We were just a dot in the China Sea. Once the ship sank we had no landmark. We 'cooeed' and a lifeboat, with some of our chaps in it, picked us up. I could have hugged them. We rowed around picking up other chaps, until our boat was filled. I remember that night. There were about seven other boats, all tied together, all filled with prisoners of war.

The Japs had come and picked up any of their lot and the girls (prostitutes) whom they had on their ships. We were left.

A terrible storm brewed—a tornado! Brigadier Varley was in one boat. The boats were banging against one another, so Brigadier Varley said, 'Every boat for ITSELF'. We cut adrift and rowed into the storm all night. I always remember rowing with a poor fellow lying on the bottom of the boat. As I rowed I pressed my foot on his stomach. I remember thinking that this poor chap would be dead in the morning. He lived! I saw him many times after the War, and he said I pumped all the water out of his stomach. His name is Stan Manning and I think he lives in Cobar NSW.

When daylight came, there was no other boat in sight. We heard machine-gun fire, but did not see anything. Those other boats had the same chance as we did. I think the Japs machine-gunned them in the morning but I have no proof.

We rowed around all day trying to find the others but saw no one. The next day we started to head for the China coast. Frank McGovern and Dr Rowley Richards were our main navigators. We eventually ran into another lifeboat and we exchanged English POWs for Australians. That is how I ended up with Rowley Richards, Russ Savage, Ian McDiarmid and Jimmy Mullens. We had a blanket for a sail. We seemed to be making good time. We only had about 400 miles to go to get to the China coast.

The next day we saw a destroyer or frigate approach us. We did not wish to be picked up by the Japs again. We did not know if we would be shot or not. Anyhow, it was Japs and they came alongside us and asked if we were Dutch. We said 'Yes'. We felt they thought we were Germans.

They picked us up and packed us forward on to the bow of the ship. It was terribly hot. They gave us a cup of water but I could have drunk a bucketful! We had been in the water for two days without anything before we got picked up in the lifeboat and then we spent a day and a night in the lifeboat before the Japs picked us up.

That night we passed a large ship that was still burning and had not yet sunk. We went right past it.

My tongue was terribly swollen. I could hardly speak. A chap lying beside me said, 'Here Dig, wet your mouth, some of the other chaps are'. Even though we had been put on our word not to touch our water rations I swilled my mouth out and got my tongue working again. I told this chap that when we got home I would buy him the biggest beer he had ever drunk. He said, 'What's your name, mate?' I said, 'Loughnan'. He said, 'Not Kitch?' I said, 'Yes'. He told me he'd been looking for me in Burma. His name was Laurie Looke. He managed Brighton Downs for J.W. Fletcher. Betty and May Fletcher had told him to look out for me.

We were taken to the island of Hainan. We were placed on a tanker which was a terrible sight. A lot of English were trying to get out of the heat and into the shade, by crawling under pipes on the deck of the tanker. Their sockets were raw! They had lost their eyes in the sea when it was alight with fuel. We washed out their sockets with the salt water and pulled kapok out of life jackets to fill them. I do not think I have seen men in a worse mess.

Jim Mullens said to me, 'Let's jump over and swim to the coast'. We just did not have the guts to do so. Anyhow before dark and before we could think any more we were transferred to a big ship used as a whaling factory. We were safer on that as the tanker we had been on was full of fuel. We were put down in the holds of the whaling factory and bolted in. I did not think Hell could be any worse than down there. We sailed for Formosa.

They fed us down in the holds. There was very little water, no baths and no toilets! It was terrible!

Every day we would hear explosions. We never knew if we were torpedoed or not. We started off in quite a large convoy. Not so many ships arrived in Formosa. Most were sunk. We were one of the few that got through.

One night in particular I remember so well. There was a terrific explosion. One chap, a petty officer, went up on top, somehow. I was lying beside Dr Rowley Richards. The petty officer told us that we had been torpedoed again but we should make land. We felt dreadful. We thought, not again! Rowley and I were lying down and I said to Rowley, 'See that post, it is too upright for us to be listing too much'. Rowley said, 'Yes, I think so too. I have been watching that post too.' As it turned out we were not hit.

At Formosa we were formed into another convoy which made two or three attempts to get to Japan. We were chased back each time by the Americans. We eventually got under way and I think we were the only ship out of that convoy to reach Moji in Japan. We were taken off the whaler and taken to a 'dip' between the two islands of Honshu and Kyushu. These 'dips' were two wooden tubs about ten feet by ten feet. We were just shoved into them and pushed under like sheep. Puss and excreta floated on top of the water! You were forced to hold your nose and keep your mouth shut while you were pushed under! Afterwards we had to put the same clothes back on. You can imagine mine, a filthy pair of underpants, nothing else.

We were marched on to a bitumen parade ground at Moji where we had to sit for about half a day. Most of us still had dysentery or malaria. We had to just sit there, no toilets or anything to wipe our bottoms with. At least, in the jungle, we could use leaves. At dark we were taken to a hall and given a meal—the first meal we had had since landing.

Next day we were drafted into parties. We were marched through a big town, I think Tokyo. Here the Japs issued us with some clothes. You can imagine—secondhand Jap clothes that did not fit. We did get one good Moji blanket and a great coat, which helped to save our lives. We were marched along corridors . . . I do not know if we went from island to island, but we seemed to go for miles. We were put in a train and taken across one suburb to another and then put on another train. This time we were put in carriages—the first time we had ever had anything to sit on. I'll never forget it. We were given a *binto* box containing rice, a piece of fish and two grasshoppers, which was our meal that night. It never hit bottom!

After quite a long journey north we arrived at a place called Sakata on the west coast. We were put in one big hut with a twenty-foot wooden wall around us. There we remained camped until we were released. We were so far north in Japan we were nearly opposite Vladivostock in Russia.

There were no beds, only boards. We had only a sort of kapok eiderdown to keep us warm. The cold got to 36 degrees below zero. I do not think any place could have been worse! The cold was nearly too much, especially as were not clad for it. It was nothing for men to collapse on the parade ground. We worked from daylight until dark, rain, hail or snow. The Japs loved to get us up about midnight to search us for radios or such. Out we would be stood on the parade ground, in snow or sleet.

We had three main jobs to do—timber stacking, loading sawn timber and carting coal. To cart the coal we were given a sort of straw waistcoat to wear. We then had large boxes lifted on to our backs. These boxes had a trapdoor at the bottom. We would walk into the barges and another chap had to shovel the coal into the boxes on our backs. Often he missed and the coal went down between the box and our backs. It was awful, especially when the coal was covered in ice.

The other job we had was in the smelting works where there were big vats of boiling metal. One thing, we could get warm doing this job. One day a chap by the name of Jasper Swartz and I were carrying huge bottles of spirits of salt. We could hardly carry them, they were so big and heavy, also we were so emaciated. Jasper fell and broke a bottle. A Jap hit him with a timber spike in the back. We carried Jasper back to the hut—he died that night! I volunteered to go back to Japan after the War to make certain that murdering Jap paid for Jasper's death. They never sent me. So much accounted for! So many Jap guards got off free. They were murdering bastards.

The third job was just as bad. They were going to kill us somehow through work, starvation or murder. There were thousands of big logs tied together, some of the logs being about forty feet long and two to three feet through. They were held together by a big one-inch cable. We worked nearly twelve months there taking logs off and one could hardly see where we had started. We had a crane on the logs lifting them out of the water and on to the land. We would then have to roll them up into railway trucks. The blizzards coming in from Siberia were terrific. We cried with the cold. Titch Leimen was the main man on the crane. I still owe him for a packet of cigarettes I think. We have not seen one another since.

20

The beginning of the end

AT noon on 15 August 1945, the people of Japan heard for the first time in history the sacred voice of their Emperor. All over the country tense groups of soldiers and citizens gathered around hastily erected loudspeakers and a great hush displaced the sounds of a nation at war.

On that day I was working with fellow prisoner of war Walt Ditteaux, an American marine, in a lumberyard at Fukuoka carrying shingles from one stack to another. All morning our *hanchos* had displayed an uncharacteristic lack of concern about our slovenly attitude to the job and about midday left us altogether to crowd around a large loudspeaker mounted above the office door. A disembodied voice came over the air waves and before long we were astonished to observe tears streaming down some of the guards' faces. After what seemed a very long time, the voice died away, but our guards and *hanchos* remained still as if suddenly struck dumb and immobile. After a while they rounded us up and silently marched us back to camp.

In prisoner of war camps all over Japan similar incomprehensible ceremonies were taking place.

Of all the cities in Japan, Hiroshima and Nagasaki had world wide prominence thrust upon them in August 1945 following the dropping of the atomic bombs. Within two kilometres of the epicentre of the blast over Nagasaki on 9 August 1945, POW

Camp 14 had been flattened, with four of its inmates killed and 30 injured. Miraculously all 24 of the Australians in the camp survived, and with Dutch and British survivors worked for days on rescue, salvage and clearing up in the devastated city. Being such a centre of world interest ensured that the Americans and international press gave it the highest priority.

Sergeant Peter McGrath-Kerr, 2/40th Battalion, who was injured in the bomb blast, has recorded his last days at Nagasaki.

On 19 August the POWs were paraded before the Camp Commandant and told that the War was over. The men showed little emotion, probably because the ordeal through which they had been made them apathetic and they could raise no enthusiasm. Work parties ceased from then on. Several days later some Mitchell bombers flew low over the barracks so we arranged plywood panels on a level open area to spell 'POW'. On 31 August an American bomber with 'PW Supplies' painted under the wings flew over the camp, turned away and flew back overhead and dropped containers with parachutes. These were full of food and were recovered by the prisoners of war helped by some of the local Nipponese. Apart from some Red Cross supplies which had been brought in by ferry about a week before, this was the first lot of European food which we received.

Our Nipponese guards left us on 2 September and the prisoners of war took over the camp administration. The guards gave us a month's food and some rifles to protect ourselves, but I couldn't see the need for these as the Nipponese people showed no hostility to us in the barracks area.

On 7 September an American war correspondent came into the camp. He had arrived in Japan with American troops who had landed at the airfield at Kanoya, and he told us that if we could get to Kanoya we would be able to get a lift to Okinawa in one of the supply planes which were returning empty. Next day the twenty-four Australian prisoners of war marched down to the Nagasaki railway station to catch a train to Kanoya. When we left the barracks area we took with us the ashes of the Australians who had died in Fukuoka 14. These had been given to us by the Nipponese authorities after we moved into the barracks.

The train at the railway station was crowded with people, but the stationmaster cleared part of one carriage so that we could be seated.

The railway line ran along the Urakami valley and as we travelled along we could see the devastation which the bomb had caused. Past the factory area trees were dead on the side facing the bomb blast. The train journey took two days, with an overnight stop at a railway station, name not known. Here we slept in the waiting room after the station staff had supplied us with dixies of cooked rice and other food, but what sort it was I cannot remember now. After changing trains several times we arrived at Kanoya railway station in the dark. On the platform were some American MPs who arranged for trucks to take us to the airfield which the American forces had occupied. Jack Marshall and myself, both having an arm in a sling, were taken to the camp hospital and put to bed after the hospital staff had questioned us with great interest in our experiences.

Next day, 10 September, ex-prisoners of war were flown to Okinawa where we were issued with new clothing, American Army type, and accommodated in a tented camp. I was taken to an American Army hospital and X-rayed to find the extent of my injuries. The plates showed that five ribs on my right side had been fractured, as were three small bones in my left had, one of the bones knitted out of alignment, so the fingers would not bend because the tendon was trapped in the callus formation.

Chief Petty Officer John King of HMS *Exeter* was one of the longest prisoner of war residents of Nagasaki, Camp 2, having arrived there in October 1942. The *Exeter* had been sunk in the battle of the Java Sea on 1 March 1942 together with HMS *Encounter* and USS *Pope*. On 13 October 1942 John King sailed from Macassar with about 250 Royal Navy and American Navy personnel and 1000 Dutch and Indonesian prisoners of war on the *Asama Maru*. He was in Fukuoka Camp 2 at Nagasaki when I arrived there in a party of 200 Australians in September 1944 and was still there when the atomic bomb exploded eight kilometres distant over the city of Nagasaki. He wrote:

On 9 August 1945, I was on the bridge of the ship at the 'big' dock watching a B-29 circling Nagasaki when there was this almighty flash like lightning, then an orange explosion, then the blast. I was thrown right across the bridge, covered in dust and glass, and a

151

couple of my mates took me to the big air-raid shelter in the dockyard.

After the bomb dropped everything was chaos, but we still had to work in the dockyard, and things were very cagey. We had been told that 'when the first American lands on Japan, first we shoot all prisoners, then women and children commit suicide, and we fight to the last man', so that it was touch and go at that time.

We really didn't know what had happened at Nagasaki—you know the stories they used to tell us—you couldn't believe a word they said, and when I was told that one bomb had killed 100 000 people and that Nagasaki had just disappeared I could only say 'bullshit'.

We finished work on 14 August 1945 and things were very tense everywhere, and on 15 August the first things we wanted were the rifles and ammunition. When we had those we were reasonably safe—although you know what kind of bastards they were, they could turn on us at any time, and there were only about 500 of us with about fifty rifles.

Things got sorted out and Boko Go, the sergeant, was the one to watch. It was C.P.C. Thomson—HMS *Encounter*—Chief of Room 4, who could bully him, who took control of the guards and handled everything. The Americans dropped us food and clothing, but we were forbidden to leave the island, after the officers discovered about the atomic bomb. But of course we had to have a look for ourselves, so that I caught the ferry twice up to Nagasaki, but twice was enough—it was devastated, and the smell was awful even weeks after the drop.

Not only was it awful to see, but some of the survivors were living skeletons, and it was only then that I realised what had happened! I had seen Southampton and Plymouth bombed in England—rubble, bricks, concrete and dust everywhere in a bomb raid which may have lasted an hour—but to see a whole city which had been devastated in about ten seconds was unbelievable, and of course, as I have said one did not know how some fanatical Japs would act.

After the surrender of Singapore, when the 'old *Exeter*' was one of the few ships left at Java, and [after] the bombings which we had to take from December 1941 until we were sunk on 1 March 1942, then [after] Macassar, Fukuoka 2, Nagasaki, then the atomic bomb, was it worth sticking my neck out, or stay in the camp?

I remember one evening—there were not many of us British left in the camp—I was walking with two of my pals—'Ginger' Black and Dougie Gray—we were all from Glasgow, Scotland. Dougie said, as [we] were looking out at the little village across from the camp, 'Do you think that we will ever make it?' 'Ginger' Black was honest when he said, 'I really don't think so'. I said, 'Well, we have been lucky so far'.

John King returned home and was still thriving when I last heard from him five years ago.

21

Liberation in Mukden

B Y May 1945 most prisoners of war in Manchuria had been concentrated near Mukden where some 2000 were gathered. The Russians' declaration of war on Japan on 8 August 1945 and the rapid advance of their troops into Manchuria ensured earlier liberation of Allied prisoners there than of those in Japan. Flight Lieutenant C.H. ('Spud') Spurgeon, 8 Squadron RAAF, who had been shot down and captured in Malaya in 1941, was one of them.

Rumours of impending liberation reached Mukden as early as 10 August. On 6 August, although we did not know at the time, the first A-bomb was dropped on Hiroshima; three days later the second was dropped on Nagasaki. The Russians declared war on Japan on the 8th and speedily marched into Manchuria. On 15 August the men returned at lunch time from the factory—an unprecedented happening!

At about 11.30 a.m. on the 16th, when I was walking in the quadrangle with Air Vice Marshal Maltby, Air Officer Commanding in Chief, we noticed a four-engined aircraft (as it turned out, a B-24) flying low over the airfield to the north of the camp. It was an unusual event, as none of us had ever seen a Japanese four-engined aeroplane! Then we noticed several parachutes, white ones, followed by several red ones on the second pass.

Parties of prisoners from No. 1 and No. 2 Branch camp outside Mukden were coming into our main camp all afternoon. At 4.30 p.m. the word came that a strange group of four white men and

154

two orientals were talking to Japanese, near the guard-house. They were neither bowing nor saluting and still wore side-arms. After supper they were noticed sitting in the Commandant's office, the officer in charge of the party still wearing a pistol and smoking a large cigar! Nobody slept that night.

After breakfast on the 17th the senior US, British and Dutch officers were summoned to the Commandant's office to be told that Japan had surrendered to the United States, Great Britain and China but not to Russia. We were to stay where we were for the time being under Japanese protection. The parachute party was from Chungking and comprised Major Hennessy, Major Lamar (a doctor), Corporal Leith who spoke Russian, a radio corporal, a Nisei interpreter and a Chinese interpreter.

In the meantime we could hear sounds of gunfire and rioting outside the camp walls and the occasional explosion and bullets whistling above our heads, so we were content to stay where we were!

On the evening of 20 August we were attending a concert put on by our camp 'orchestra' when a call came for three senior officers and Sergeant Hurley, a prisoner who also spoke Russian, to report to the main gate. When we got there we found several Russian officers, the spokesman for whom was Captain Elim Gehtman, standing on the hospital steps with the three senior officers.

Gehtman's speech in Russian was translated by the interpreter thus:

'Gentlemen of the Allied prison Camp: In the name of the Russian Red Army I proclaim that from this moment you are free. (CHEERS! and more CHEERS!) Russia entered this war ten days ago. Since that time we have marched across country, over hills and valleys and where there were no roads for more than 1000 kilometres and have arrived victoriously. I congratulate the United States, Great Britain and Allied nations on this great victory and for releasing the world from Japanese oppression.'

The captain then asked if General Wainwright was present. When told that he was still at a northern camp, General Parker, the senior US officer present, then stepped forward and said:

'I am sure I speak for all of you when I express our thanks and appreciation to the *Imperial* Russian Army and congratulate them on their great victory.'

And that was probably not the first time that particular *faux pas* was committed!

155

The Russians then marched eleven Japanese officers and some thirty other ranks into the centre of the square, where they were disarmed. The Russian captain called for a guard detail from the prisoners, who were then armed with Japanese weapons, and marched the Japanese officers to their quarters and the other ranks into the guardhouse.

On the evening of 18 August the Russians arrived in singular fashion—by driving a tank straight through the wall! Whether it was an error of judgement is doubtful as the entire crew appeared to be, to put in mildly, 'under the influence', including one gentleman who was wearing what appeared to be a very lurid pair of pyjama trousers over his uniform, and brandishing a bottle of vodka. He announced that we were free to go into town as we wanted.

Thus began a period of incredible and zany activity. On one excursion into town we located a warehouse full of bottled beer which we proceeded to load into the local horse-drawn cabs or '*droshkis*' to transport back to camp. Several visits were paid to the brewery, until our efforts were dramatically terminated when a Russian who objected to what we were doing blatantly shot one of the horses and drove us away. The beer, however, was mild in strength and very enjoyable while it lasted.

A further hazard while wandering around the city was the insistence by usually extravagantly intoxicated Russians that victory should be celebrated with them by downing tumblers full of raw vodka, an activity calculated to produce a significant effect on stomachs unused to such treatment.

On other occasions, time was spent in the French consular residence of Monsieur Renner, the main attraction being his charming wife, and more particularly his teenage daughter! My schoolboy French was never very good, but it was certainly better than their English, and adequate for the moment.

Other contacts were made with the civilian internees who had been held in the Mukden Club. They included a group of Jesuit priests, one of whom, Father Dom, a Belgian, who like me happened to be a keen philatelist, accompanied me on a visit to the Post Office where we obtained samples of postage stamps, including overprints which had been hastily improvised to celebrate the Allied and Chinese victory. These purchases were facilitated by the issue of local currency which had been advanced to us by the residents' Rescue Group at the camp.

On 24 August the first group of prisoners departed when two B-24s took out thirty-two hospital patients, one of whom was Oscar

Diarmond. Subsequently, these movements were heavily restricted because of the comparative shortness of the runway, but not before the senior generals including Generals Percival, Wainwright and others over the rank of brigadier had also been air-evacuated. Some 300 were ultimately repatriated this way.

By the time August turned into September we were beginning to feel desperate and to wonder when we were to be relieved. Efforts were made to alleviate our concern; more equipment was shipped in, we were briefed by a visiting Press Relations party—one even acknowledged the Australian contribution in New Guinea—and our entertainment included a visit by a Russian entertainment party, whose dancers, acrobats and musicians were a source of unaccustomed pleasure.

In the meantime, our visits to the city became less frequent, as the Russians restored order. Visits were made to the local airfield where a Russian group attack squadron had moved in. We were amazed to see so many women pilots among the crews, some obviously decorated. Their more obvious social advances were graciously declined however.

We had almost daily visits from B-29s whose bomb bays opened overhead and literally showered us with supplies. I have never seen so many Mars bars and neither had the kids in Mukden, who dived in the adjacent swamp to recover them. A photograph I obtained after the war shows a bag of cocoa exploding as it penetrated the roof of, I think, the camp mortuary.

Eventually on 9 September word came that US ships awaited us at Talien (Dairen) better known to prewar geography students as Port Arthur. The Russians at last arranged two trains to take us there. I was in the first party, some 750-strong, but before we left we were fumigated and inoculated, presumably to part us from the company of the fleas and other vermin to which we had become hosts over the years. On 11 September we were loaded into trucks and taken to the station where we boarded a very crowded train. We carried American 'K' rations with us and at each stop these were supplemented with fruit, eggs and local food given by the Chinese. We finally left Mukden at about 6 p.m. on a journey normally scheduled at eight hours, but which was eventually to take twenty-six. The scenery en route was interesting, particularly at one stop where we drew up alongside a Russian troop train. Outside our window, on a low-bed railway car, was a four-ton flat truck complete with mattress and several 'ladies' dressed in Russian uniform and of ample proportions, whose contribution to the war effort was never doubted! And again all seemed to be in the usual incredible inebriated condition.

It was dark when we finally reached the marshalling yards at Talien, and to conclude the railway circus this journey had been the locomotive promptly ran off the rails! We disembarked and with our kitbags slung on our backs moved off towards a glow we could see atop the wharfside sheds. To our delight, when we finally arrived on the wharf, there was the most beautiful sight, a lovely white hospital ship, a huge Red Cross on the funnel, fully illuminated and with her name emblazoned on her side in lights. It could hardly have been more appropriately named—US Navy Hospital Ship *Relief*.

The sight of the clean uniforms, very attractively turned-out nurses, who looked to us like Hollywood film stars, and the subtle whiff of perfume were as much as a lot of us could stand! We were bathed, shaved, issued with clean pyjamas and put to bed with a cup of hot chocolate. I have never slept so soundly or restfully as I did on that night. But the journey home was not over yet.

In addition to the hospital ship, a Landing Ship Infantry (LSI) by name USS *Colbert* tied up at the wharf. Four destroyer escorts were anchored nearby. These latter ships on departure from Talien preceded the two ships carrying POWs to surface and destroy by gunfire those mines that appeared in our path. As each mine exploded it was a pretty sight, especially when the ships' searchlights illuminated the explosion.

After two or three days we were anchored in Buckner Bay in Okinawa. We had not been there long, however, and had only unloaded the sickest of our passengers when a typhoon warning was issued. Hastily we of the *Relief* got under way; the wind had strengthened and many of the smaller ships and craft were pitching into heavy seas. For two days we stayed at sea, in some of the fiercest winds and roughest seas imaginable. The ship practically ran out of food and I well remember one meal when all that was served was canned tomatoes and ice cream!

Finally we returned to Okinawa on 16 September. Evidence of the force of the storm was apparent everywhere. Two or three large ships had been thrown up on the beach and countless small vessels wrecked or sunk. The airfield camp where we stayed overnight had also suffered quite severe damage and many parked aircraft were wrecked or badly damaged.

After a short period of negotiation with a US pilot I managed to include myself in the passenger list on a very dilapidated C-46 aircraft whose crew were going to the Philippines. I can remember staring apprehensively at the stain of a large engine oil leak as it spread over the mainplane and wondering what would happen if the crew had to manage this heavily overladen beast on one engine! We landed at Nielsen Field in Manila on 18 September, from where we were transferred at first to the 29th Replacement Camp and thence to 5 Replacement Depot where No. 3 Australian PW Reception Group had been established to process all returning Australian prisoners of war. Still the frustrating delays continued! Either the Reception Group had orders to delay our departure or it was simply a shortage of transport to Australia—there was no urgency to move us out. The camp was comfortable enough, we had stretchers in duck-boarded tents, the food was good, and we had access to grog, cigars, and candy bars. Entertainment was provided to keep us amused, but nobody seemed to understand that all we wanted to do was to get home to our families and friends.

Finally an Airforce officer arrived in the camp to supervise evacuation by air and very quickly an aircraft was requested from Morotai to take the small group of RAAF to Darwin. Almost secretly, on the morning of 1 October, we were driven to Clark Field and embarked on a Liberator—its number was A72-116—which landed in Darwin at about 2.30 p.m. My joy and excitement at landing there was reinforced by one of my original flying-course mates greeting me with a frosty cold bottle of beer—a typically Australian welcome!

Two days in Darwin followed. And more questioning, more medical examinations, and, finally and coincidentally a visit to Easy Arm near Darwin, where I met once again my old course captain at Point Cook, who just happened to be CO of a Catalina squadron. The RAAF group of eleven, plus five Army 'odds and sods' left Darwin next morning at 5.30 in a Catalina (A24–82) for Cairns, where we spent the night of 5 October in an Army hospital, to Brisbane on the 6th to spend the night at Sandgate in the RAAF personnel depot and so on to Sydney, landing at Rose Bay at noon on 7 October. Lunch with my sister-in-law followed and on that evening we left by train for Melbourne. My best recollection of that trip was the comparative comfort of the wire-mesh bunks and the magnificent cup of hot coffee at Seymour Station in the early morning! At Spencer Street Station we were quickly whisked into buses and to the Melbourne Cricket Ground—an RAAF Personnel Depot. Believe it or not I entered that famous arena through the same gate as Bradman did, to walk the 300 yards across the hallowed ground to be greeted by my sister and her family. I was home.